Felt Wee Folk

ENCHANTING PROJECTS

Salley Mavor

C&T PUBLISHING

Dedicated to Anne, a sister who still shares her imagination

To my husband, Rob Goldsborough, for his constant support and encouragement; my sons Ian and Peter for helping to keep things in perspective; my parents Mary and Jim Mavor for instilling a sense of wonder and believing in the value of art; Judy Richardson for first writing The Way Home and years later helping with this book; Judy-Sue Goodwin-Sturges for her enthusiasm and friendship; the parents and staff at the Waldorf School of Cape Cod; Ed and Kathleen Smith of Textile Reproductions; Carol Chittenden of Eight Cousins Children's Books; and Tom Kleindinst, Emily Sper, and Doug Mindell for their beautiful photographs.

©Salley Mavor 2003

Editor-in-Chief: Darra Williamson
Editor: Cyndy Lyle Rymer
Technical Editor: Sara Kate MacFarland
Copyeditor/Proofreader: Pam Mostek
Cover Designer: Aliza Shalit
Design Director/Book Designer: Rose Sheifer
Production Assistant: Kristy A. Konitzer

Published by C&T Publishing, Inc., P.O. Box 1456, Lafayette, California 94549

Front cover: *Puppy Play* by Salley Mavor (see page 71), photo by Doug Mindell

Back cover: *Driftwood Clan* (page 50), *Blossom Fairy* (page 34), *Cat Pin* (page 57)

Title page: *Sleeping Fairy*, photo by Doug Mindell

Library of Congress Cataloging-in-Publication Data
Mavor, Salley.
  Felt wee folk : enchanting projects / Salley Mavor.
    p. cm.
  Includes index.
    ISBN 1-57120-193-9 (paper trade)
  1. Dollmaking. 2. Felt work. I. Title.
TT175 .M385 2003
745.592'21--dc21

2002014870

Printed in China

10 9 8 7 6 5

Contents

LAVENDER

A Journey into the Wee World

This book is about sewing by hand in a playful, fanciful way, with an eye toward the natural world. It is an invitation to those of us who take delight in little things and keep a collection of buttons, beads, and other interesting "stuff" with the thought that these treasures will be put to good use some day.

We spy the little curved doorway at the foot of a tree. We can't help but take a closer peek at the soft patch of moss tucked between the roots and imagine the comings and goings of the little people who must live there. Acorn caps become hats and a walnut shell serves as a tiny cradle. Young and old are welcome to enter this delightful world of creative play.

In this book I've presented little dolls that might inhabit an enchanting miniature scene, from flowery Blossom Fairies to a fully outfitted Driftwood Clan Pirate. You'll find step-by-step instructions for constructing different-sized bendable doll bodies with painted wooden bead heads. With the basic wrapped-wire form as a foundation, an unlimited assortment of characters and personalities can come to life with wool felt and faux (or silk) flower petal costumes.

In addition to the Wee Folk, there are many examples of pins, purses, balsam pillows, and appliquéd scenes, all hand sewn with wool felt and accented with beads and buttons. The designs

DANDELION, doll and photo by Salley Mavor

make use of small pieces of wool felt and found objects, as well as provide boundless opportunities for embellishment.

The ideas presented are for needleworkers of all ages and skill levels, from the beginner who is learning the blanket stitch to the experienced embroiderer who relishes fine stitching. There is plenty of room for adapting the design details. The goal is not so much to make perfect fancy stitches as to explore the possibilities of working with a needle and thread, to have stitches serve a utilitarian purpose and be beautiful at the same time.

All of the projects pictured in this book are made with 100 percent wool or wool-felt blend, some commercially dyed and some plant dyed. The experience of working with genuine, natural materials such as wool felt is heavenly. Quality supplies are worth the extra cost and effort for the sheer pleasure of handling them and for the integrity of the finished product. I've included a source list on page 78 to help seek out some hard-to-find materials.

I hope that the little dolls and other felt projects pictured in the chapters ahead will inspire people of all ages and sewing abilities to gather some interesting bits and pieces and start cutting, wrapping, and stitching in a spirit of fun and freedom.

ROSEHIP

Once Upon a Thread

My mother's hands were always busy working on projects. As a five-year-old, I remember watching her sew a real-looking fur collar and cuffs onto a doll's coat. The coat was gray and wooly on the outside and the inside was dotted with little hearts. There was even a matching fur-trimmed hat with ribbons to tie under the doll's chin.

My parents created a home full of art, music, and dance. We were surrounded by an international array of handmade crafts and the sounds of ethnic music, anything from pulsating Bulgarian melodies to French-Canadian fiddle tunes. In our household it was clear that making art was more important than housework. My mother was always willing to involve my sister, brother, and me in whatever craft technique she was working on at the time, whether it was making paper maché puppets, throwing a pot on the wheel, or painting hot wax on cloth to make batiks. Art supplies were abundant, and there was a sense that time was always available for creative pursuits.

When I was a little girl, my sister and I spent countless hours creating a miniature world with our toys and found objects. Scraps of cloth, old buttons, snaps, and eyehooks made clothes, accessories, and furnishings for our dolls. Sewing snaps onto tiny felt outfits was my passion. Our measure of excellence was in the impeccable doll clothes sewn by our southern great aunts, Dell and Alma Salley.

SALLEY AT RISD, 1977, photo by Emily Sper

Any pieces of cloth left lying about fell victim to my eager scissors. My mother even discovered a small square cut out of her shower curtain. Somehow, I didn't think a tiny piece would be missed, and my doll needed that shiny plastic in her custom bathroom.

We covered the old oak table in the basement with a roofless one-floor ranch house for Barbie and our troll dolls. I remember trying to make Barbie sit in a natural position, but all she could do was stick her legs out straight, pointing her pitiful little high-heeled feet. The trolls, on the other hand, were stable and grounded in their homely squat bodies. The doll table was a major interest for many years, until the onset of adolescence when our continued attraction to dolls became an embarrassing secret.

Then my mother taught me to sew on her Singer Featherweight ™. In my 4-H club, the Harborview

STUFFED PINS, 1979

Sewers, lime green culottes were my proudest accomplishment. In high school I made a garish quilt from fabric scraps and old dresses, and knit an Icelandic sweater with circular needles. I learned some embroidery stitches from a book and decorated my friends' blue jean shirts and bell-bottoms with flowers. I felt confined by patterns and grids and preferred to experiment on my own, making mistakes and trying again.

It wasn't until years later, while studying illustration at the Rhode Island School of Design (RISD), that I started to sew and make dolls again. After struggling through a watercolor class, I came to understand that I would never be an illustrator in the traditional sense. The bewildered instructor was at a loss for words when I showed him my work. Little paint was visible under the layers of pastel, cut paper, and polka dot stickers. At this point I regarded my paintings and drawings not as finished pieces but as a starting point from which to launch an idea, like scenery behind the show. The impulse to add textures and objects was so compelling that I found myself only interested in creating work that had a three-dimensional element.

It was wonderfully refreshing to hold different materials in my hands and let intuition guide me.

I was aware of a tactile connection to the creative process, much like the synergy of play. It was such a relief to find out that I was free to communicate my ideas in three dimensions and still be an illustrator.

Encouraged by my teacher, Judy-Sue Goodwin-Sturges, I continued to experiment with dollmaking and found objects, learning techniques and processes on my own.

By my senior year I was making dolls of all kinds, animals and people with movable limbs, and setting them up in scenes to be photographed. My senior thesis was a series of scenes from Hansel and Gretel, complete with a gingerbread house baked in my little apartment oven.

REFRIGERATOR, 1979

After graduation in 1978, I made and sold a line of stuffed fabric pins, designed sewing projects for women's magazines, and worked on a series of housewife dolls and their stuffed appliances. In an effort to have my work recognized more as art than handiwork, I decided to adapt my technique to a relief format so it could be presented in a frame.

I had seen some seventeenth-century stump work at the Victoria and Albert Museum in London and was inspired to try something similar, which I called "fabric relief." Since I had no idea how the old stump work was actually made, I explored ways of covering cardboard with fabric and forming people, animals, and buildings sewn onto a fabric background.

My husband, Rob Goldsborough, made beautiful wooden shadow box frames for the new work. I welcomed the added challenge of making

SHOPPER, 1980

FEEDING CHICKENS, 1986

telling a story. I was ready to try illustrating a children's book. Some editors in New York found my work interesting but too idiosyncratic to fit with any story they had on file. Later, my friend Judy Richardson and I went to New York together, as writer and illustrator, and sold *The Way Home* to a publisher.

We went prepared, bringing a storyboard, sample illustrations, and a 4" x 5" transparency to show how the work would look when photographed. I was not so prepared for the lengthy task of filling a thirty-two-page book with pictures. For a year and a half, after my boys went to bed in the evening, I would sew the elephant characters and hand embroider blades of grass. When the book was published in 1991, Judy and I were as proud as new parents. This was the beginning of a decade of illustrating six picture books, including *Come to My Party*, another elephant story by Judith Benét Richardson.

When I consider a manuscript, I read it through, noticing if the story evokes strong imagery and has clear, definable characters, elements that can help focus my attention throughout the process. The classic poem, *Mary Had a Little Lamb*, was an opportunity to create a

environments for the figures, keeping a three-dimensional quality to their magical, miniature world behind the glass.

Motherhood saved me from fully escaping into the world of my imagination, where life is a manageable and controlled fantasy. My idealistic dream of working at home, while the children played happily beside me, quickly fizzled. The real demands of caring for two lively little boys brought me down to earth, but I remained determined to find time to work on my art. I learned to be efficient with short windows of time, focusing on my work like a horse with blinders.

For several years I experimented with fabric-relief sculpture, dyeing fabric, wrapping wire, adding found objects, and constructing wooden scenery parts. I wanted to bring grace and a sense of movement to the static figures through exaggerated gestures. More and more, my work was turning into miniature, shallow stage sets, with scenery, props, and characters

Illustration from *IN THE HEART* ©2001 by Salley Mavor, used with permission from Harper Collins

Illustration from *MARY HAD A LITTLE LAMB* by Salley Mavor ©1995, Orchard Books, photo by Tom Kleindinst

nineteenth-century New England landscape. The adventure of selecting poems and making a variety of children in seasonal environments in *You and Me: Poems of Friendship*, kept me engrossed in the project. Real live plants and blue water dyed with food coloring enhanced the fantasy garden scene in Martin Waddell's, *The Hollyhock Wall*. In my most recent picture book, *In the Heart*, by Ann Turner, I was charmed by the little girl character and aimed to surround her with a loving family and friends.

In between book projects, I like to put aside all deadlines and work on one-of-a-kind pieces just for myself. Some of my favorites were constructed with items saved by my late grandmother who, in her 96 years, hardly ever threw anything out. Some of the things she left behind would normally have been considered worthless and discarded without a thought. To me the drawers and boxes filled with old sewing supplies, hairpins, costume jewelry, and

garter clips were as precious as treasure chests filled with sparkling jewels. I think she would be pleased to know her things were being put to good use.

When I became involved in my children's Waldorf School, it made me more aware of the value of creative and imaginative play in the classroom and in life. Our school's parent handwork group introduced me to the wonderful wool felt and fleece that is now a staple ingredient in my artwork. I shared examples of little people and other small felt projects I had made and taught parents how to make them. Working with the group, I had to learn how to break up the technique into steps and explain methods in a way that was not overwhelming.

Since I am self-taught in needlework and have an intuitive, experimental approach to my work, it is a challenge for me to dissect the creative process into logical parts. I know that many people like to have an idea of what a project will end up looking like, have all of the materials at hand, and have clear directions to follow. With this in mind, I decided to put together an acorn-capped fairy doll kit and launched a business named Wee Folk Studio.

Recently I have been photographing various fairies, transporting them in a basket looking for suitable natural settings. Friends drive by and catch me out on a hazy day, taking pictures at local marshes, gardens, and beaches. Strangers don't see the little fairies and think that I'm just photographing flowers. My sons are embarrassed to see me at their high school, gathering acorn caps from under oak trees, bending over with a basket on my arm, "like a peasant woman," as my son Peter says. I suppose I am destined to become even more eccentric as time goes on, but I am comforted by the knowledge that creating art keeps my imagination alive and makes me feel whole and happy.

GEORGE'S CHAIR, 1998, photo by Doug Mindell

Illustration from *YOU AND ME: POEMS OF FRIENDSHIP* by Salley Mavor ©1997, Orchard Books, photo by Tom Keindinst

HYDRANGEA

PORCELAIN BERRY

MERMAID

LILY PAD TWINS

13

Gathering Materials

Many of the materials used to make the projects in this book, like chenille stems, unvarnished wooden beads, embroidery thread, faux flowers, and acrylic paint, are readily available from craft and needlework stores. Obtaining some supplies, such as wool felt, wool fleece, balsam fir, nail heads, and glass beads will require seeking out mail-order companies and online businesses that sell these items. Refer to the list of suppliers in Sources (page 78). Some of the best supplies, though, are right under your nose or outside under a tree. Sift through boxes of old trinkets or gather acorn caps, shells, and other natural wonders from outside.

Salvaged, interesting items can add a distinctive personal touch to a project.

FAUX FLOWER PETALS

Faux Flowers

I've made the *Blossom Fairy's* skirts from faux or artificial flowers, which are sometimes referred to as silk flowers. Most flowers found in craft stores are not real silk but synthetic. Pull the blossoms apart from the stems and other plastic parts and save the individual fabric petals. I rearrange the flowers in different combinations to form the circular layers of a skirt. Look for flowers that are the right diameter, color, and shape for a fairy's costume. Those that work well for this purpose are dahlias, zinnias, asters, and daisies, which have multiple petals radiating from the center. Flowers with unique shapes, such as roses and daffodils, do not work well for this purpose.

Fairy wings are made from freesias and lilies, which have long petals tapered to a point. Cut one petal off from the grouping of three, leaving two joined pointed petals that look like wings.

FAIRY WINGS

FLORA AND ROSEBUD

PINK IVY IN GRAY TREE

Acorn Caps

I make the little hats that top off the fairies and Wee Folk from caps separated from acorns. The best time to collect caps is in the fall, when mature acorns have fallen from oak trees. You can find acorns not just on the forest floor, but also on the sidewalks of city streets lined with oak trees. The variety of oak trees that grow in different parts of the country produce acorn caps that range in size from 1/4" to 1 1/4" diameter.

There are subtle but important differences in the shape and depth of the acorn caps, with some better suited for little hats than others. Certain caps are too shallow and flat inside to conform to the shape of a bead head, and others are so deep that the doll's face disappears inside. The curve inside the cap should fit naturally onto the doll's bead head, leaving a little extra room for fleece hair. Some caps have a fine textured pattern, some have tiny bumps, while others have sharp spikes. Acorn caps that are harvested early and brought inside to dry out will last a long time and do not need to be sealed with varnish. If you live in a part of the country where there are no oak trees, enlist the help of scavenging friends and relatives who live where there are acorns.

ACORN CAPS

Wool Felt and Fleece

There are different types of felts, some made from 100 percent wool fibers and others made from a blend of wool and rayon. Craft felt is made from synthetic fibers and contains no wool. Depending on the manufacturer, wool felt varies considerably in thickness, can be commercially dyed in bright,

saturated colors, or plant dyed in more subtle shades. Most of the projects in this book were made from plant-dyed wool/rayon felt and plant-dyed fleece. Carded and dyed wool fleece makes nice natural-looking hair for the Wee Folk. Fleece should never be cut with scissors. Instead, the fibers can be gently pulled apart with the fingers.

Balsam Fir

For aromatic pillows, use dried balsam fir tips gathered and processed in Maine. Their attractive woodsy fragrance will last at least five years.

Projects for Children to Make

These projects are fun and easy for children to make. They are simplified adaptations of the Wee Folk, fairies and felt purses featured in this book. Some children with sewing experience and fine dexterity can move on to the more complicated, wrapped versions of the little people.

Flower Fairy

Materials

* 12''-long, 3mm diameter chenille stem for body
* 12mm unvarnished wooden bead for head
* Acorn cap to fit the bead head
* Wool fleece for hair
* Small piece of green felt for tunic
* 5 faux flower parts for skirt
* One set of faux flower petal wings
* 16" length of size 3 perle cotton
* Large-eye needle
* Colored pencils for facial features
* White glue

BODY Bend the chenille stem in half and use the illustration as a guide to shape the arms and legs. Twist the two wire ends together at the neck.

LAYERED FAIRY SKIRT

COMPLETED FAIRY

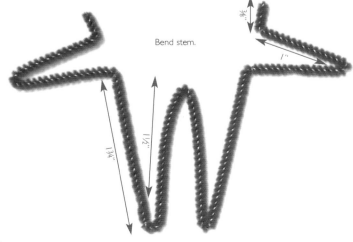

Bend stem.

3⁄8"

1"

1 3⁄4"

1 1⁄2"

FAIRY TUNIC Use the pattern to cut out the fairy tunic. Poke the fairy's neck through the hole in the tunic and arrange the front and back over the body. Sew twice through the felt top at the waistline from front to back using the attached thread to form a belt. The third time around, in the front, bring the thread up to the neck, wind it around once, and then bring the thread through to the back. Sew the wings to the back with a few small stitches.

FAIRY'S TUNIC

FAIRY'S TUNIC
Cut one.

Layer flower petals by size.

SKIRT Arrange the flower petals from small to large.

Squeeze the two legs together and, starting with the smallest petal, slide each flower petal up to the top of the legs. If necessary, cut small slits out from the center to enlarge the flower's center opening. The skirt layers should fit snugly or they will fall down. Thread and knot the Perle cotton and sew a few stitches through the top of the fairy's skirt keep it in place. Do not cut the thread but continue on to the next step.

FAIRY WINGS

HEAD Use the colored pencils to draw a face on the bead. Glue the wooden bead onto the fairy's neck and let it dry. Spread glue on top of the head and then drape the fleece hair over the head to attach it. Spread a little glue inside the acorn cap and place on top of the head.

Wee Folk Boy or Girl

Materials for one doll

* 12''-long, 3mm diameter chenille stem for body
* 14mm unvarnished wooden bead for head
* Acorn cap to fit the bead
* Small felt pieces for clothing
* Embroidery floss
* Embroidery needle
* 4'' length of size 3 perle cotton for belt
* Colored pencils to create facial features
* White glue

For girl

* Wool fleece for hair

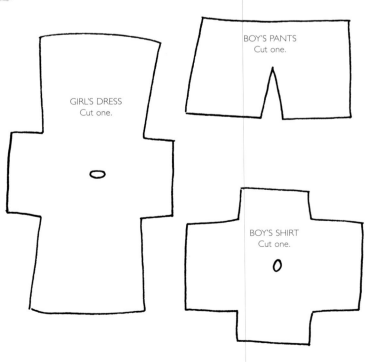

BOY

GIRL

CLOTHING Use the patterns to cut out the pants and shirt or the dress. Fold the pants legs toward the center and with two-ply floss, blanketstitch up and down the inside seam. Slide pants up the doll's legs and sew closed at the back and top, securing with a few stitches so that the pants won't fall down.

Poke the doll's neck through the hole in the shirt or the dress and position the front and back over the arms and body. Use two-ply floss to blanket stitch the arm and side seams together. Tie perle cotton around the girl doll's waist to form a belt. Bend the doll's feet.

HEAD Use the colored pencils to draw a face on the bead. Glue the bead head onto the doll's neck and let it dry. For the girl doll's hair, spread glue on top of the head and then drape the fleece hair over the head. Spread a little glue inside the acorn cap and place on top of the head.

BODY Bend the chenille stem in half, then use the diagram as a guide to shape the arms and legs.

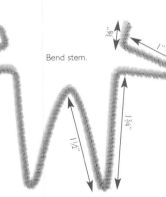

Bend stem.

3⁄8"

1"

1¾"

1½"

Twist the two wire ends together at the neck.

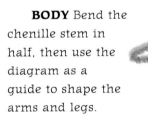

WIRE BODY

PANTS

Clothing Patterns

GIRL'S DRESS
Cut one.

BOY'S PANTS
Cut one.

BOY'S SHIRT
Cut one.

Felt Purse

CAT PURSE

Materials

* 3½" x 9" piece green wool felt for purse
* 2½" x 3" piece orange wool felt for cat
* 2 small green glass beads for eyes
* Embroidery floss: yellow, orange, and black
* Embroidery needle
* Yellow size 3 perle cotton
* Green sewing thread
* Large sew-on snap

1. Pattern Pieces

Cut out the cat pattern piece on page 22. Cut out a 3½" x 9" piece of felt for the purse, slightly rounding the corners on one end.

2. Sew on the Snap

Fold the felt purse piece one-third of the length and pin in place. Using the green thread, sew the snap socket to the purse outside and the stud to purse inside, being careful not to have the threads show on the outside. Hide knots under the snap.

CAT PURSE

4. Attaching the Cat to the Purse

Unfold the purse; pin the cat onto the outside of the front flap. Use two-ply orange floss to blanketstitch the cat to the purse around the cat's outer edge, hiding knots between the cat and the purse flap.

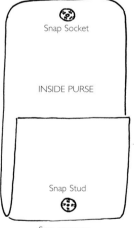

Snap Socket

INSIDE PURSE

Snap Stud

Sew on snaps.

Snap Stud

OUTSIDE PURSE

Sew cat to purse flap.

3. Decorate the Cat

Use all six strands of yellow floss to stitch stripes in a zigzag pattern on the cat's back and satinstitch the cat's nose. With one-ply black floss, sew the bead eyes in place. Stitch a black line down the center of each eye to make the stitches look like pupils. Stitch the cat's mouth and whiskers with the black floss.

5. Stitching the Purse

To form the purse pocket, fold the felt piece at one-third of the length and pin in place. Use Perle cotton thread to blanketstitch through the double thickness, from point A to point B. Stitch along the pocket's single-layer edge from B to C and again through the double thickness from C to D. Then blanketstitch around the purse flap edge from point B to point C. Hide knots inside the purse pocket.

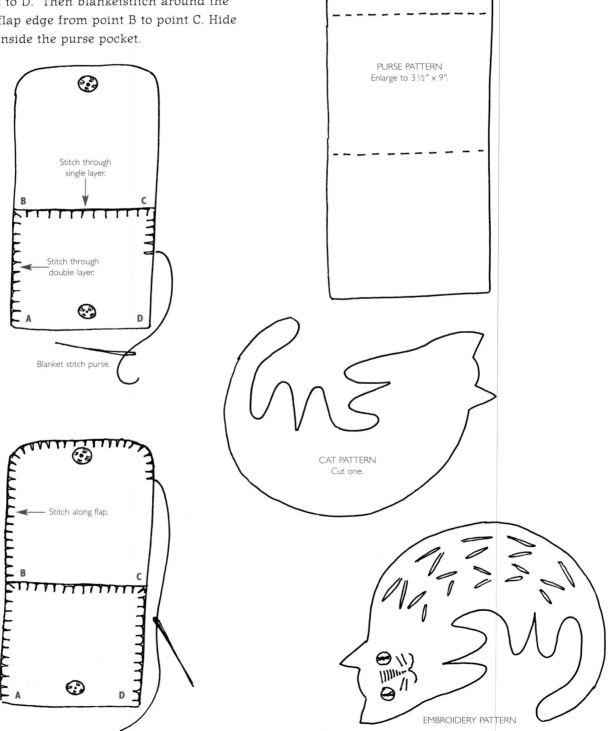

PURSE PATTERN
Enlarge to 3½" × 9".

Stitch through single layer.

B   C

Stitch through double layer.

A   D

Blanket stitch purse.

Stitch along flap.

B   C

A   D

CAT PATTERN
Cut one.

EMBROIDERY PATTERN

PURPLE POSY

Making Wee Folk and Fairies

I've made the Wee Folk and Fairies pictured throughout this book from basic armatures of wrapped chenille stems, painted wooden bead heads, and clothing sewn from wool felt. To make fairy skirts and wings, I pull apart faux flowers and rearrange them. The following directions show how to make different sized figures, from the tiniest 1½" baby to a full-size 4" pirate. Each size is shown with step-by-step instructions for making a sample doll. You can use the various doll armatures to create the Wee Folk or fairies that are shown in detail in the chapters ahead. *Since the dolls include small parts, they are not intended for children under 3 years of age.*

Materials

* 3mm (thin) or 6mm (regular) chenille stems for bodies
* Unvarnished wooden beads for heads
* Acorn caps to fit the bead heads
* Wool fleece for hair and fairy's torso
* Wool felt pieces for clothing
* Faux flower petals for fairy skirts and wings
* Embroidery floss
* Embroidery needle
* Acrylic paint for faces
* White glue

NOTE: Specific sizes for chenille stems, bead heads, and acorn caps are listed with the individual project directions.

BEAD
HEADS

Tips for Body Wrapping

To wrap the chenille stems, keep the embroidery floss in the original skein wrapper and pull out a few feet of thread to start. Don't cut the thread, but continuously pull out more from the skein as needed. For the smoothest wrapping, keep the thread from twisting into a tight spiral. Untwist and flatten out the six strands of floss so the threads fan out, and the floss evenly covers the chenille "fuzzies."

Basic Instructions

FACE PAINTING Fold a chenille stem in half and slide bead heads onto it so they don't roll around while painting. Cover the entire bead with a skin-color acrylic paint. Paint the white of the eyes, then make a dot in the center for the eye color. Use a small pointed brush and a darker shade of brown to paint the eyelids, nose, and mouth. Paint the cheeks and lips with a rosy shade.

CLOTHING Use the patterns provided for each doll to cut out clothing pieces from felt. Pinking shears can be used to cut a zigzag edge on some pattern pieces. Stitch decorations onto the clothing with embroidery floss. Add bead buttons and any other embellishments that strike your fancy.

PANTS: Blanketstitch lower pant leg edges. Fold the outer pant edges to the center and stitch up and down the center and inseams. Put the pants on the doll by placing the legs into the pant legs. Secure at the back and waist with a few stitches so the pants won't fall down.

SHIRT OR DRESS: Blanket stitch the sleeve, lower edges, and neckline opening. Add desired embellishing to the garment front. Poke the doll's neck through the center hole and position the front and back over the doll's arms and legs. Blanket stitch the side seams together from the sleeve to the hem.

ATTACHING THE HEAD, HAIR, AND ACORN CAPS
Attach the bead head to the body with a dab of white glue on the wire neck. Let the glue dry before proceeding. *Glue guns do not work well for this project. White craft glue holds better and is less stringy.* For a girl, spread glue on top of the bead head to attach the wool fleece hair. Drape the fleece hair on top, with long tresses hanging down on the sides. For a boy, spread glue on top of the bead head and then wrap fleece around the crown of the head. Spread glue around the inside cup of the acorn cap and place it on the top

BOY
(Larger than actual size)

of the head. After the glue is dry, the hair can be braided or shortened by pulling and breaking apart the fibers with your fingers.

FAIRIES For a fairy skirt, select four or five different flower petals, ranging in size from large to small. Cut a set of wings from a freesia or lily flower. Cut tiny slits in the flower petals, radiating out from the center holes. Make them just big enough for the fairy's toes to fit through snugly. If the holes are too big, the flower skirt will fall down. Gently slide the petals up the legs, starting with the smallest and ending with the largest flower. For the 3½" fairy, wind wool fleece around the torso. Decorate the felt fairy tunic with embroidery stitches. Poke the doll's neck through the tunic's center hole and position the front and back over the body. Blanketstitch the side seams together from the sleeve to the waist, leaving the bottom of the tunic free to fan out. Use the same threaded needle to sew the fairy wings to the back of the tunic.

1 1/2" DOLLS AND CLOTHING

1 1/2" Doll Body

Materials

* 7 1/2"-long, 3mm diameter chenille stem for body
* 10mm wooden bead for head
* Acorn cap to fit the bead
* For a baby, use felt for clothing.
* For a fairy, use faux flower petals for the skirt and wings.

Wrapping Legs

Use the illustration as a guide to shape the chenille stem. Start by wrapping the leg-color floss tightly around the curve of the toe, covering the fuzzies.

Wrap toe.

Squeeze the two stem sections together and wrap embroidery floss up the leg, covering the thread tail. At the top of the first leg, continue winding the floss at approximately 1/4" intervals around the single stem to get down to the second toe. Wrap the second toe.

Squeeze the two stem sections together and wrap up the length of the second leg. Secure the floss with a knot by looping the floss around the top of the legs, feeding the floss through the loop and pulling tight. Trim the floss, leaving a 2" tail.

Wrap second toe.

Wrapping Arms

Wrap the arm-color floss tightly around the curve of a hand, covering the chenille fuzzies.

Squeeze the two stem sections together and wrap floss along the length of the arm, ending at the center of the body. Continue wrapping the floss at approximately 1/4" intervals around the single stem to get over to the second hand. Wrap floss around the curve of the second hand.

Wrap hand.

Wrap second hand.

Squeeze the stems together and wrap along the length of the second arm back toward the torso. After completing both arms, wind floss around the base of the neck. Tie a knot with the leg floss tail and trim the thread.

Secure wrapping threads together.

Finishing

Follow the basic instructions for making the clothing and attaching the head, hair, and cap.

2¹/₂" Doll Body

Materials

* 12"-long, 3mm-diameter chenille stem for body
* 12mm or 14mm unvarnished wooden bead for head
* Acorn cap to fit the bead
* Wool fleece for hair
* For a fairy skirt and wings, use artificial flower petals.

2¹/₂" DOLL

Boots

Use the illustration as a guide to shape the chenille stem. Wrap the boot-color floss tightly around the curve of the toe, covering the chenille fuzzies.

Wrap boot.

³/₈"

1"

1³/₄"

¹/₂"

Squeeze the two stem sections together and wrap up the length of a boot (about ¹/₂"). Secure the floss by looping it around the boot top, feeding the floss through the loop and pulling tight. Trim the floss, leaving ³/₄" tail. Repeat for the second boot.

Anchor threads at boot top.

Legs

Start at the top of one boot and wrap up the length of the leg with the leg-color floss. Cover the thread tail and fuzzies as you go.

At the top of the first leg, don't cut the floss but continue winding at approximately ¹/₄" intervals around the single stem to get down to top of the second boot.

Squeeze the two stem sections together and wrap up the length of the second leg. Knot the thread at the top and trim, leaving a 2" tail.

Wrap leg above boot.

Travel floss to second leg.

Arms

Wrap the arm-color floss tightly around the curve of a hand.

Squeeze the two stem sections together and wrap floss around the length of the arm.

Continue wrapping the floss at approximately ¹/₄" intervals around the single stem of the second arm to get over to the hand. Wrap floss around the curve of the second hand.

Wrap hand.

Wrap second hand.

Squeeze the stems together and then wrap around the length of the second arm back toward the torso. After completing both arms, wind floss around the base of the neck a few times. Wind the floss around the middle of the body, tie a knot with the leg floss tail, and trim the thread.

Secure arm and leg threads.

Clothing and Head

For a fairy, slip on a flower petal skirt as described in the Basic Instructions for Fairies on page 25.

Follow basic instructions for making clothing and attaching the head, hair, and acorn cap.

FELT TOP

FAIRY WINGS

FAIRY SKIRT

Layer flower petals by size.

3" Doll Body

Materials

* 6mm-diameter chenille stems for body: One 11"-long for legs, one 10"-long for arms
* 16mm unvarnished wooden bead for head
* Acorn cap to fit the bead
* Wool fleece for hair
* Wool felt pieces for clothing

3" DOLL

Boots

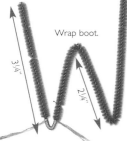

Wrap boot.

3/4"

2 1/4"

Use the illustration as a guide to shape the chenille stem. Wrap the boot-color floss tightly around the curve of the toe, covering the chenille fuzzies.

Wrap second boot.

Squeeze the two stem sections together and wrap up the length of a boot (about 1/2"). Secure the floss by looping it around the top of the boot, feeding the floss through the loop and pulling tight. Trim the floss, leaving a 3/4" tail. Repeat for second boot.

Legs

Start at the top of one boot and wrap up the length of the leg with the leg-colored floss. Cover the thread tails and fuzzies as you go.

At the top of the first leg, don't cut the floss but continue winding at approximately 1/4" intervals around the single stem to get down to top of the second boot.

Squeeze the two stem sections together and wrap up the length of the second leg. Knot the thread at the top and trim, leaving a 2" tail.

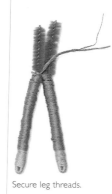

Wrap leg.

Wrap second leg.

Secure leg threads.

Arms

Fold the 10"-long stem in half. Use the illustration as a guide to place the bent center between the legs and twist around the middle section of the body, leaving a 3/4" section at the top for the neck. Bend the arm sections as shown. Wrap the arm-color floss tightly around the curve of a hand. Squeeze the two stem sections together and wrap floss around the length of the arm. Bend the extra stem end around the body midsection. Continue wrapping the

Wrap hand.

floss at approximately ¼" intervals around the single stem to get over to the second hand. Wrap floss

Wrap second hand.

around the curve of the second hand.

Squeeze the stems together and then wrap around the length of the second arm back toward the torso. Bend the extra stem end around the body midsection. After completing both arms, wind floss around the base of the neck a few times. Wind the floss around the middle of the body. Tie a knot with the leg floss tail and trim the thread.

Secure leg and body threads.

Finishing

Follow the basic instructions for making the clothing and attaching the head, hair, and cap.

FELT DRESS

3 ½" DOLL

3½" Doll Body

Materials

* Two 12"-long, 6mm-diameter chenille stems for the legs and arms
* 16mm unvarnished wooden bead for head
* Acorn cap to fit the bead
* Wool fleece for hair
* Wool felt pieces for clothing
* Seed beads for buttons
* For a fairy, faux flower petals and wings

Boots

Use the illustration as a guide to shape one chenille stem.

Wrap the boot-color floss tightly around the curve of the toe, covering the chenille fuzzies. Squeeze the two stem sections together and wrap up the length of a boot (about ½"). Secure the floss by looping it around the top of the boot, feeding the floss

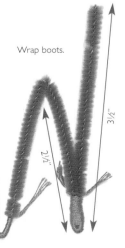

Wrap boots.

2½"

3½"

through the loop and pulling tight. Trim the floss, leaving ¾" tail. Repeat for second boot.

Legs

Start at the top of one boot and wrap up the length of the leg with the leg-color floss. Cover the thread tail and fuzzies as you go. At the top of the first leg, don't cut the floss but continue winding at approximately 1/4" intervals around the single stem to get down to the top of the second boot.

Squeeze the two stem sections together and wrap up the length of the second leg. Knot the thread at the top and trim, leaving a 2" tail.

Travel floss to second leg.

Wrap second leg.

Arms

Fold the other 12"-long stem in half. Use the illustration as a guide to place the bent center between the legs and twist around the

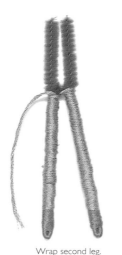

½"   1⅜"   ¾"

Wrap hand.

Wrap second hand.

body midsection, leaving 3/4" at the top for the neck. Bend the arm sections as shown. Wrap the arm-color floss tightly around the curve of a hand.

Squeeze the two stem sections together and wrap

floss around the length of the arm. Bend the extra stem end around the body midsection. Continue wrapping the floss at approximately 1/4" intervals around the single stem of the second arm to get over to the hand. Wrap floss around the curve of the second hand.

Squeeze stems together and wrap around the length of the second arm back toward the torso. Bend the extra stem end around the body midsection. After completing both arms, wind floss around the base of the neck a few times. Wind the floss around the body midsection. Tie a knot with the leg floss tail and trim the thread. If desired, crisscross contrasting thread up and down the legs.

Wrap legs.

Finishing

For a fairy, slide flower petals up the legs and wind wool fleece around the body midsection.

Layer flower petals by size.

Wind fleece around body.

Follow the basic instructions for making clothing and attaching the head, hair, and acorn cap on page 25.

TUNIC AND WINGS

4" Doll Body

Materials

* Two 12"-long, 6mm-diameter chenille stems for the legs and arms
* 20mm unvarnished wooden bead for head
* Acorn cap to fit the bead
* Wool fleece for hair
* Wool felt pieces for clothing

Boots

Use the illustration as a guide to shape one chenille stem. Wrap the boot-color floss tightly around the curve of the toe, covering the chenille fuzzies.

4" DOLL

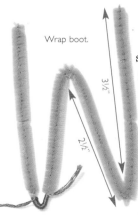

Wrap boot.

3½"

2½"

Squeeze the two stem sections together and wrap up the length of a boot (about ½"). Secure the floss by looping it around the top of the boot, feeding the floss through the loop and pulling tight. Trim the floss, leaving ¾" tails. Repeat for the second boot.

Wrap second boot.

Legs

Travel floss to second leg.

Start at the top of one boot and wrap up the length of the leg with the leg-colored floss. Cover the thread tails and fuzzies as you go. At the top of the first leg, don't cut the floss but continue winding at approximately ¼" intervals around the single stem to get down to top of the second boot.

Squeeze the two stem sections together and wrap up the length of the second leg. Knot the thread at the top and trim, leaving a 2" tail.

Arms

Fold the other 12"-long chenille stem in half. Use the illustration as a guide to place the bent center between the legs and twist around the stem ends to make the body midsection. Bend the stems to form what will be the arms and neck. Wrap the arm-color floss tightly around the hand curve.

Secure threads.

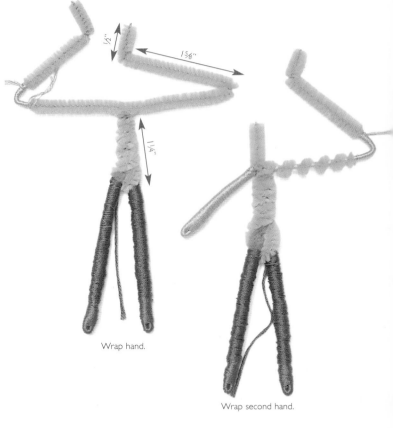

½"

1⅝"

¼"

Wrap hand.

Wrap second hand.

Squeeze the two stem sections together and wrap floss around the length of the arm. Continue wrapping the floss at approximately ¼" intervals around the single stem to get over to the second hand. Wrap floss around the curve of the second hand.

Squeeze stems together and then wrap around the length of the second arm back toward torso. After completing both arms, wind floss around the base of the neck a few times. Wind the floss around the body midsection. Tie a knot with the leg floss tail and trim the thread.

Wrap fleece body.

Finishing

Wrap wool fleece around the body midsection. Follow the basic instructions for making clothing and attaching the head, hair, and acorn cap.

FELT CLOTHING

BUD AND IVY

SWAMP ROSE

Blossom Fairies

M ake a collection of fairy dolls, from the tiniest 1½" baby to a mature 3½" fairy. Construct their wrapped wire bodies (see pages 24, 26–32), and dress the fairies in bright petal petticoats and embroidered wool felt tunics. Sew on a pair of wings made from faux freesia or lilies. Paint a face onto a wooden bead and glue the head onto the neck. Glue on wool fleece hair and an acorn cap to finish the doll. Once the glue dries, she's ready to fly!

2½" DOLL, 12MM HEAD

2½" DOLL, 14MM HEAD

3½" DOLL, 16MM HEAD

3" DOLL, 14MM HEAD

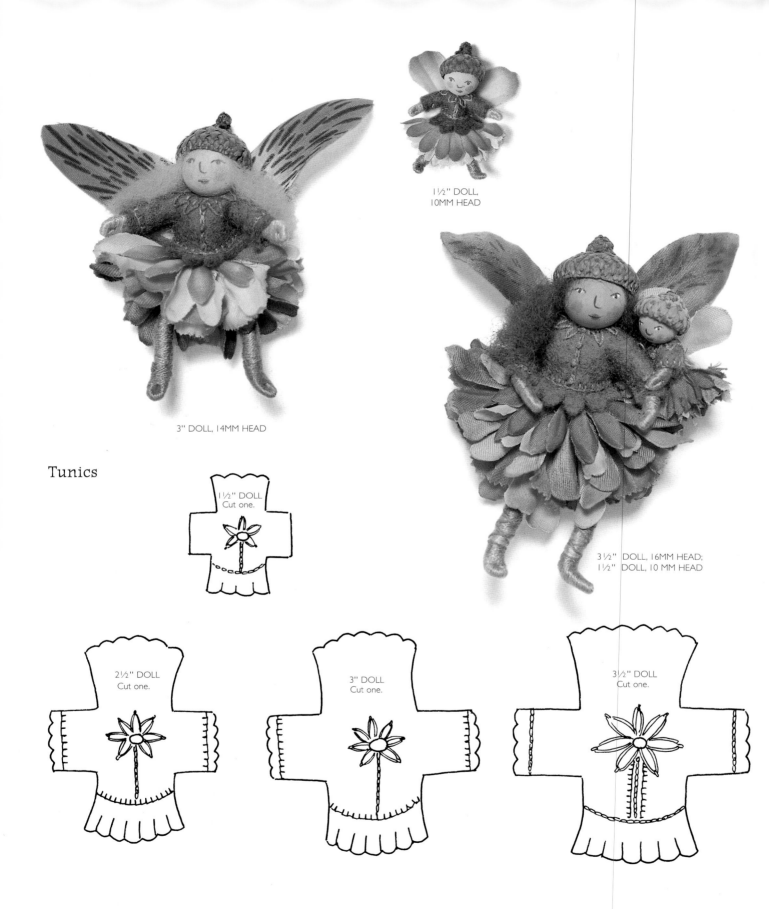

1½" DOLL,
10MM HEAD

3" DOLL, 14MM HEAD

3½" DOLL, 16MM HEAD;
1½" DOLL, 10 MM HEAD

Tunics

1½" DOLL
Cut one.

2½" DOLL
Cut one.

3" DOLL
Cut one.

3½" DOLL
Cut one.

Hansel and Gretel

ost in the woods, this delightful Hansel and
Gretel find a gingerbread house decorated with entic-
ing candy. To create this charming pair, refer to the
materials listed below and to the photograph for
color selection, costume possibilities, and decoration
ideas. Clothing patterns are on page 38. Follow the
basic clothing instructions on pages 24-25.

Hansel and Gretel

Materials

* Two 3'' doll armatures (page 28)
* Two 16mm unvarnished wooden beads for heads
* Wool fleece for hair
* Wool felt pieces for clothing
* Metallic seed beads for buttons
* Embroidery floss
* Embroidery needle

Witch

Materials

* 4'' doll armature (page 31)
* 20mm unvarnished wooden bead for head
* Wool fleece for hair
* Wool felt pieces for clothing
* Metallic seed beads for buttons

GRETEL, 3" DOLL

HANSEL, 3" DOLL

WITCH, 4" DOLL

Hansel and Gretel Clothing Patterns

Gathering line

WITCH'S SKIRT
Cut one.
4" doll

WITCH'S TUNIC
Cut one.
4" doll

GRETEL'S DIRNDL
Cut one.
3" doll

GRETEL'S BLOUSE
Cut one.
3" doll

HANSEL'S SHIRT
Cut one.
3" doll

WITCH'S APRON
Cut one.
4" doll

WITCH'S HAT
Cut one.

HANSEL'S HAT
Cut one.

HANSEL'S SUSPENDERS
Cut two.

HANSEL'S LEDERHOSEN
Cut one.
3" doll

GRETEL'S BONNET
Cut one.

CROSSPIECE
Cut one.

HANSEL AND GRETEL, photo by Doug Mindell

Royal Family

$\mathcal{S}$hiny metallic thread and gold acorn cap crowns help make the king, queen, prince, and princess look impressively regal. In addition to the immediate royal family, a court of characters including a jester, knight, and wizard add to the medieval entourage. The following materials are for the different costumes for each figure in the sandcastle scene. Patterns for the dolls' clothing are on pages 44-45. Follow the basic clothing instructions on pages 24-25.

Materials

* Metallic thread
* Gold or silver spray paint

Wind metallic thread around the arms and legs after the dolls' armatures have been wrapped with embroidery floss. Crisscross the thread up and down, making a pattern on top of the original layer of floss wrapping. Use a combination of embroidery floss and metallic thread to decorate the felt clothing with embroidery stitches. Spray paint the acorn caps, covering only the outside, since glue will adhere better to the unpainted inside surface.

QUEEN, 4" DOLL

KING, 4" DOLL

King
Materials

* 4'' doll armature (page 31)
* 20mm unvarnished wooden bead for head
* Acorn cap to fit the bead
* Wool fleece for hair
* Wool felt pieces for clothing
* Shiny thread for belt

Queen
Materials

* 4'' doll armature (page 31)
* 20mm unvarnished wooden bead for head
* Acorn cap to fit the bead
* Wool fleece for hair
* Wool felt for clothing
* One faux flower for skirt

ROYAL FAMILY, photo by Doug Mindell

Prince

Materials

* 3½'' doll armature (page 29)
* 16mm bead unvarnished wooden bead for head
* Acorn cap to fit the bead
* Wool fleece for hair
* Wool felt pieces for clothing

PRINCE, 3½'' DOLL

Princess

Materials

* 3½'' doll armature (page 29)
* 16mm unvarnished wooden bead for head
* Acorn cap to fit the bead
* Wool fleece for hair
* Wool felt pieces for clothing
* Faux flower petals for skirt

PRINCESS, 3½'' DOLL

Knight

Materials

* 4'' doll armature (page 31)
* 20mm unvarnished wooden bead for head
* Wool fleece for hair
* Silver metallic fabric for chain-mail hood
* Wool felt for clothing
* Leather strip for belt
* Metallic thread for lacing legs and arms

KNIGHT, 4'' DOLL

Jester

Materials

* 4'' doll armature (page 31)
* 20mm unvarnished wooden bead for head
* Wool fleece for hair
* Wool felt pieces for clothing
* Size 3 perle cotton for belt
* 13 metallic seed beads
* Two 5mm metallic beads for hat

JESTER, 4" DOLL

Wizard

Materials

* 4'' doll armature (page 31)
* 20mm unvarnished wooden bead for head
* 6'' x 6½'' piece blue wool felt for wizard's robe and hat
* Silver or gold stars and small, round nail heads
* White sheepskin, fleece, or faux fur for beard
* Size 3 perle cotton thread for belt

To attach the nail heads to the robe and hat, push the prongs through the felt and use needle-nosed pliers to bend them over on the underside.

WIZARD, 4" DOLL

KING'S TUNIC
Cut one.
4" doll

QUEEN'S TUNIC
Cut one.
4" doll

CAPE
Cut one for king.
Cut one for queen.
4" doll

Gathering line

QUEEN'S SKIRT
Cut one.
4" doll

WIZARD'S ROBE
Cut one.
4" doll

WIZARD'S HAT
Cut one.
4" doll

WIZARD'S BEARD
Cut one.

Harvest Folk

Dressed in the colors of fall, these Wee Folk are busy gathering seeds and berries. Materials you will need for the costumes of the autumn harvest parents, children, and babies are listed below. Patterns for the dolls' clothing are on pages 48–49. Follow basic clothing instructions on pages 24–25.

Parents

Materials

* Two 4'' doll armatures (page 31)
* Two 20mm unvarnished wooden beads for heads
* Two acorn caps to fit the beads
* Wool fleece for hair
* Wool felt pieces for clothing
* Four metallic seed beads for buttons
* Embroidery floss
* Embroidery needle

PARENTS, 4'' DOLLS

CHILDREN, 2½'' DOLLS

Children

Materials

* Two 2½'' doll armatures (page 27)
* Two 12mm or 14mm unvarnished wooden beads for heads
* Two acorn caps to fit the beads
* Wool fleece for hair
* Wool felt pieces for clothing
* Size 3 perle cotton for belt
* Embroidery floss
* Embroidery needle

HARVEST FOLK, photo by Doug Mindell

Mother and Baby

Materials

For the mother

* 3½" doll armature (page 29)
* 16mm unvarnished wooden bead for head
* Acorn cap to fit the bead
* Wool fleece for hair

For the baby

* 1½" doll armature (page 26)
* 10mm unvarnished wooden bead for head
* Acorn cap to fit the bead
* For both dolls: wool felt pieces for clothing
* Embroidery floss for belt

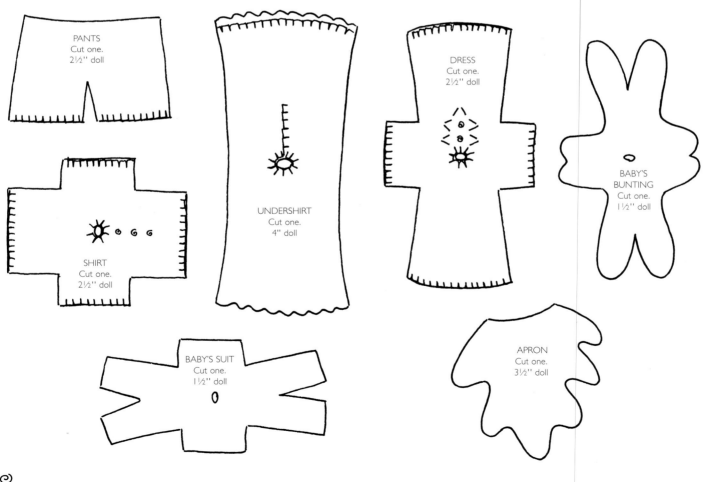

MOTHER, 3½" DOLL
BABY, 1½" DOLL

Harvest Folk Clothing Patterns

PANTS
Cut one.
2½" doll

UNDERSHIRT
Cut one.
4" doll

DRESS
Cut one.
2½" doll

BABY'S
BUNTING
Cut one.
1½" doll

SHIRT
Cut one.
2½" doll

BABY'S SUIT
Cut one.
1½" doll

APRON
Cut one.
3½" doll

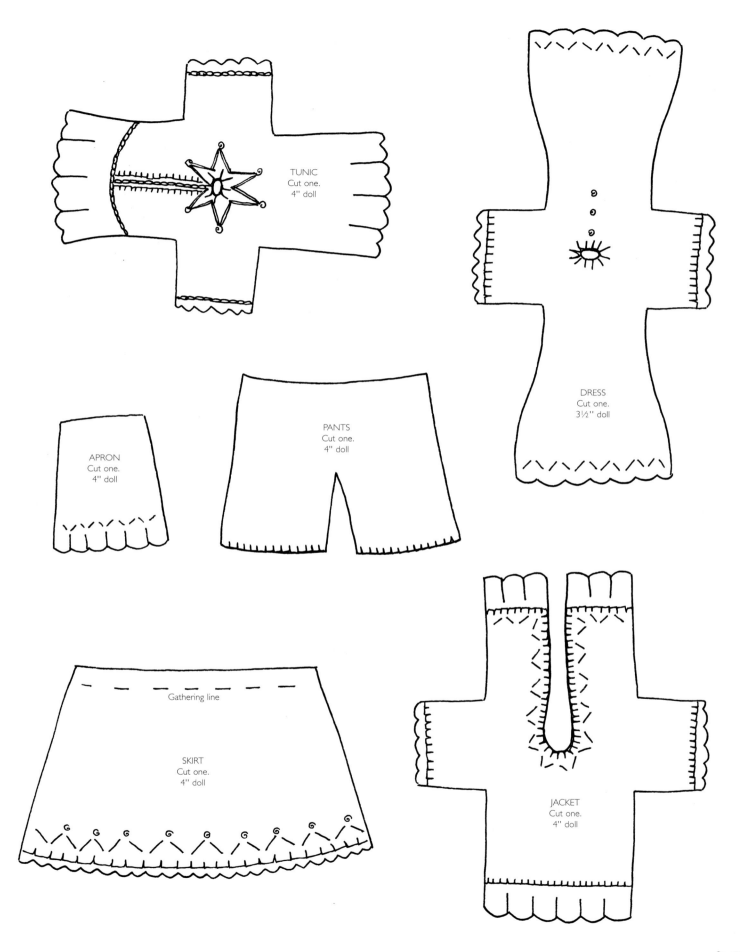

TUNIC
Cut one.
4" doll

DRESS
Cut one.
3½" doll

APRON
Cut one.
4" doll

PANTS
Cut one.
4" doll

Gathering line

SKIRT
Cut one.
4" doll

JACKET
Cut one.
4" doll

Driftwood Clan

Assembled like a large family at a reunion are several generations of Wee Folk, from young children to venerable grandparents. Even a pirate mingles with the crowd. Materials are listed below for the clan's clothing and accessories. Refer to the photograph for color selection, costume possibilities, and decoration ideas. Patterns for the dolls' clothing are on pages 53-54.

Grown-ups

Materials

* Two 4'' doll armatures (page 31)
* Two 20mm unvarnished wooden beads for heads
* Two acorn caps to fit the beads
* Wool fleece for hair
* Wool felt pieces for clothing
* Metallic seed beads for buttons

GROWN-UPS, 4'' DOLLS

Younger Children

Materials

* Two 2½'' doll armatures (page 27)
* Two 12mm or 14mm unvarnished wooden beads for heads
* Two acorn caps to fit the beads
* Wool fleece for hair
* Wool felt pieces for clothing
* Size 3 perle cotton for belt

YOUNGER CHILDREN
2½'' DOLLS

DRIFTWOOD CLAN, photo by Doug Mindell

Older Children

Materials

* Two 3½'' doll armatures (page 29)
* Two 16mm unvarnished wooden beads for heads
* Two acorn caps to fit the beads
* Wool fleece for hair
* Wool felt pieces for clothing
* Metallic seed beads for buttons

OLDER CHILDREN,
3½" DOLLS

Twins

Materials

* Two 3½'' doll armatures (page 29)
* Two 16mm unvarnished wooden beads for heads
* Two acorn caps to fit the beads
* Wool fleece for hair
* Wool felt pieces for clothing
* Size 3 perle cotton for belt

PIRATE
4'' DOLL

Pirate

Materials

* 4'' doll armature (page 31)
* 20mm unvarnished wooden bead for head
* Wool fleece for hair
* Wool felt pieces for clothing
* Metallic seed beads for buttons

TWINS, 3½" DOLLS

Driftwood Clan Clothing Patterns

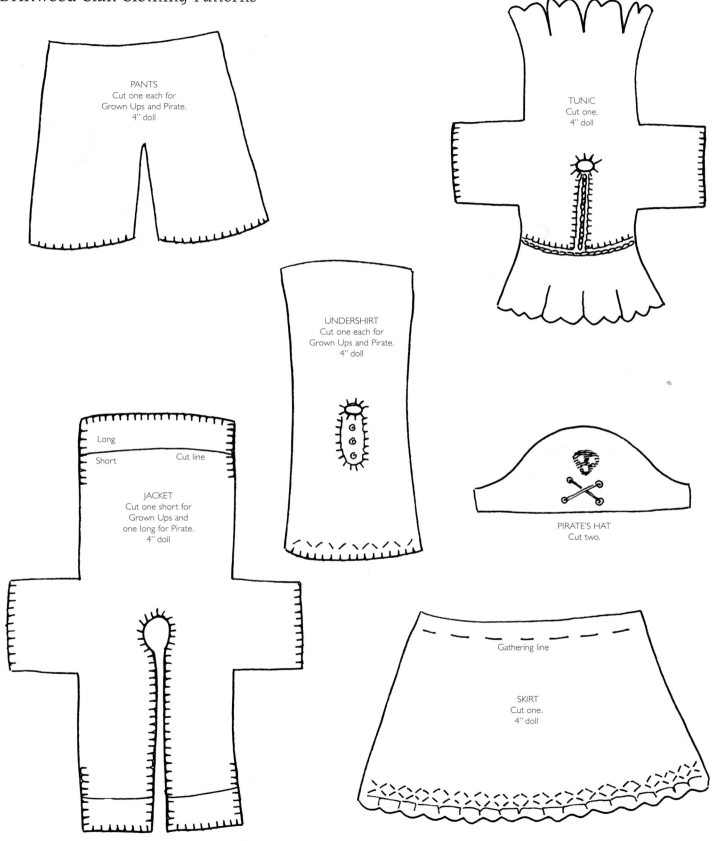

PANTS
Cut one each for
Grown Ups and Pirate.
4" doll

TUNIC
Cut one.
4" doll

UNDERSHIRT
Cut one each for
Grown Ups and Pirate.
4" doll

Long

Short   Cut line

JACKET
Cut one short for
Grown Ups and
one long for Pirate.
4" doll

PIRATE'S HAT
Cut two.

Gathering line

SKIRT
Cut one.
4" doll

DRESS
Cut one.
2½" doll

PANTS
Cut one.
2½" doll

JUMPER,
Cut one.
3½" doll

BLOUSE
Cut one.
3½" doll

SHIRT
Cut one.
2½" doll

UNDERSHIRT
Cut one.
3½" doll

PANTS
Cut one.
3½" doll

SHIRT
Cut one.
3½" doll

TUNIC
Cut one.
3½" doll

JACKET
Cut one.
3½" doll

SKIRT
Cut one.
3½" doll

Fanciful Felt Pins

These pins, made from small scraps of wool felt, with added beads, buttons, and embroidered details, can be as simple or as intricate as you want them to be. The possibilities are endless with abundant inspiration from the many small trinkets and charms that you can sew or attach to a felt background. The small scale of a pin presents a perfect setting for displaying distinctive little objects. Colorful stitches can create patterns and textures, or the smallest Wee Folk doll can be sewn onto a felt background.

The basic design consists of two layers of wool felt, with the bottom layer a bit larger to create an outer border. First, a pin back is sewn to the underside of the bottom layer. The top layer is embroidered and embellished with beads, buttons, and other objects, then sewn to the bottom layer.

To make any of the pins, follow the basic directions for the Butterfly Pin and make adjustments for shapes, materials, and stitches unique to individual pin designs. Trace the photographs of the pins on the following pages to make patterns for the top and bottom felt pieces. Refer to the photographs for colors, locations of items, and stitching ideas. Plant-dyed wool felt and a variety of cotton and silk embroidery threads were used to make these projects. *Since the pins include small parts, they are not intended for children under 3 years of age.*

Materials

* Wool felt
* 1" pin jewelry fastener
* Embroidery floss
* Embroidery needle
* Needle-nosed pliers for nail heads
* Pinking shears

ATTACHING NAIL HEADS To attach the nail heads, push the prongs through the felt and use needle-nosed pliers to bend them over on the underside.

Butterfly Pin

Materials

* Wool felt: pink and yellow
* Beads: one 16mm wooden tube; one 5mm glass; 2 seed beads
* 3" of 32-gauge cloth-covered wire
* Two small, round nail heads

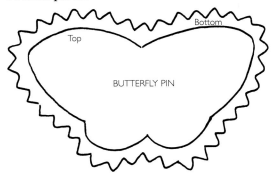

BUTTERFLY

DIRECTIONS

1. Trace the pattern for the top and bottom layers of the Butterfly Pin. Cut pieces from wool felt. Use pinking shears to cut the zigzag edge on the bottom piece.

Bottom

Top

BUTTERFLY PIN

2. Sew the pin fastener to the back of the bottom layer.

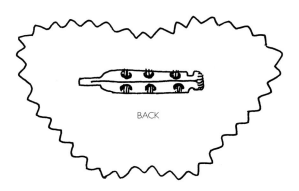

BACK

3. Attach the nail heads to the butterfly front. Use single or double strands of floss to embroider designs on the top layer with chain stitches and blanket stitches. Sew the butterfly's bead body and head in place.

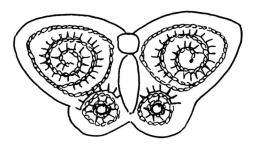

4. Bend the cloth-covered wire in half and then bend each section in half again.
5. Insert the beads onto the wire ends and slide down to rest at both bent ends.

Position beads on wire.   Twist wires.

Twist the wire sections and sew in place on the butterfly bottom layer with the two bead ends sticking out over the top and forming the antennae. Blanketstitch around the top layer outside edge to attach the top layer to the bottom layer.

Fanciful Felt Pins

STAR

Materials

* Wool felt: light green and blue
* Star button
* Seven glass "Tiny Tim Tears" beads

STAR

FRENCH KNOTTED HEART

Materials

* Wool felt: pale pink and dark pink
* Pale pink heart button

FRENCH KNOTTED HEART

OAK LEAF

Materials

* Wool felt: lavender, light green, and orange

OAK LEAF

FAIRY ON LEAF

Materials

* Wool felt: green
* 2'' fairy, with 10mm bead head and acorn cap to fit (make ½'' shorter than 2½'' doll on page 27)
* 5''of 32-gauge cloth-covered wire, folded in half and wrapped with double strands of embroidery floss

FAIRY ON LEAF

RABBIT

Materials

- ✳ Wool felt: light blue and pink
- ✳ Rabbit button
- ✳ Six aqua flat glass oval beads

RABBIT

GRAPES

Materials

- ✳ Wool felt: lavender, yellow, and green
- ✳ 19 blue, purple, or burgundy 6/0 glass beads for grapes

GRAPES

CARDINAL

Materials

- ✳ Wool felt: red and white
- ✳ Cardinal button

CARDINAL

FLOWER/BEE

Materials

- ✳ Wool felt: red and green
- ✳ Five 10mm glass red dagger beads
- ✳ Five 8mm aqua flat glass oval beads
- ✳ 10mm glass flower bead
- ✳ Metallic bee charm

FLOWER/BEE

FISH

Materials

- ✳ Wool felt: green and blue
- ✳ Three small, round nail heads
- ✳ Fish button

FISH

RED HEART

Materials

- ✳ Wool felt: blue and red
- ✳ Red heart button
- ✳ Nine blue glass seed beads

RED HEART

SCOTTIE DOG

Materials

- ✳ Wool felt: green and red
- ✳ Scottie dog button
- ✳ Seven 6mm glass lentil beads

SCOTTIE DOG

CAT

Materials

- ✳ Wool felt: pink, blue, and orange
- ✳ Two green 5/0 glass beads

CAT

Felt Appliquéd Purses

FELT PURSES, photo by Doug Mindell

The sturdy, but soft, wool felt works well for making items that will stand up to everyday use, but still feels wonderful to the touch.

To make any of the purses shown in the photograph, follow the basic directions, adjusting as necessary for shapes, materials, and stitches unique to each design. Refer to the photograph and illustrations for colors, locations of items, and stitching ideas. Small beads can be substituted for nail heads. The most frequently used stitch is the blanket stitch, with French knots, chain stitch, and herringbone stitch adding colorful details. *Because the purses have small parts, they are not intended for use by children under age 3.*

PURSE DIRECTIONS

Finished size: 3½" x 4½"

Materials

(Specific materials are listed with individual projects)

* Wool felt
* Size 16 snap fastener
* Embroidery floss
* Embroidery needle
* Size 3 perle cotton thread
* Needle-nosed pliers

Lamb Purse

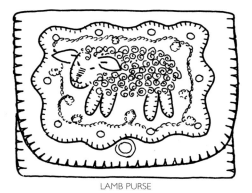

LAMB PURSE

Materials

* Wool felt: one 4½" x 10½" piece pink for purse, 3" x 3" piece white for lamb
* Ten small, round nail heads
* White Persian wool yarn

DIRECTIONS

1. **Cut Patterns and Attach the Snap** Cut the pattern pieces (page 62) out of felt. Attach snap fasteners to the purse in the positions indicated following the manufacturer's instructions.

2. **Decorate and Attach the Wool Felt Pieces** Pin the white lamb piece to the green background piece. With one-ply floss, blanketstitch around the outside edge of the lamb, tucking one ear under the head. Use one-ply floss to chain stitch the looped and wavy line around the lamb.

LAMB PURSE

Sew the lower edge of the remaining ear to the lamb. Use one-ply floss to stitch the lamb's mouth and eyes using a straight stitch and French knots. Use Persian wool yarn to make the lamb's fleece (many French knots worked close together) and satinstitch the nose on the lamb's face.

3. **Attach the Nail Heads** Push the prongs of the nail heads through the felt and use needle-nosed pliers to bend them over on the underside.

4. **Attach the Background to the Purse** Pin the background to the outside purse flap, making sure not to cover the snap socket. Use one-ply floss to blanketstitch the background piece to the purse.

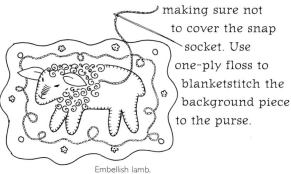

Embellish lamb.

5. **Stitch the Purse Together** Form the purse pocket by folding the felt at one-third of the length and pin to hold in place. Use a 1½-yard length of perle cotton to blanketstitch through the double thickness from A to B. Continue stitching along the single layer of felt, from B to C and again through the double thickness from C to D. Hide knots inside the purse pocket.

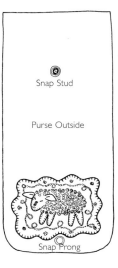

Snap Stud

Purse Outside

Snap Prong

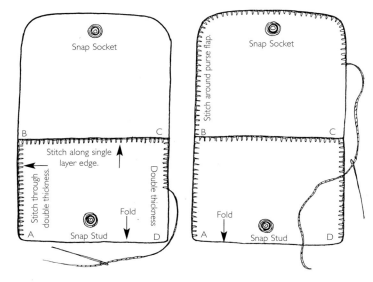

With another 1½-yard length of perle cotton, blanketstitch around the purse flap edge. Hide knots inside purse pocket at B and C.

Mitten Purse

MITTEN PURSE

Materials

* Wool felt: one 4½" x 10½" piece red for purse, one 3" x 4" piece green for background, one 3" x 3" piece red for mitten
* Two small round and two star nail heads

DIRECTIONS

Follow Step 1 on page 59.

Pin the felt mitten piece to the green background piece. Use one-ply floss to blanketstitch around the mitten outside edge. Use two-ply floss to decorate the mitten with straight stitch and French knots. Use one-ply floss to chainstitch the looped and wavy line around the mitten.

Follow Steps 3, 4, and 5 on page 59.

Straw Hat Purse

Materials

STRAW HAT PURSE

* Wool felt: one 4½" x 10½" piece light blue for purse, one 3" x 4" piece pink for background, one 3" x 3" piece yellow for straw hat
* Ten small, round nail heads
* Pink ribbon rosette

DIRECTIONS

Follow Step 1 on page 59.

Pin the yellow straw hat piece to the pink background piece. Use one-ply floss to blanketstitch around the outside edge of the hat. Use one-ply floss to embroider the hat, using chainstitch, flystitch, and satinstitch. Sew the rosette to the hat. Use one-ply floss to chainstitch the looped and wavy line around the hat.

Follow Steps 3, 4, and 5 on page 59.

Cat Purse

Materials

CAT PURSE

* Wool felt: one 4½" x 10½" piece navy blue for purse, one 3" x 4" piece green for background, one 3" x 3" piece orange for cat
* Four small, round nail heads
* Two size 6/0 green glass beads for eyes

DIRECTIONS

Follow Step 1 on page 59.

Pin the orange cat piece to the green background piece. Use one-ply floss to blanketstitch around the outside edge of the cat. Use black floss to sew the green bead eyes to the cat. Embroider the cat's face and stripes with floss. Use one-ply floss to chain-stitch the looped and wavy line around the cat.

Follow Steps 3, 4, and 5 on page 59.

Bluebird Purse

Materials

OWL PURSE

* Wool felt: one 4½" x 10½" piece lavender for purse, one 3" x 4" piece pink for background, one 3" x 3" piece blue for bird
* Five small, round nail heads

DIRECTIONS

Follow Step 1 on page 59.

Attach a nail head to the bird piece for the eye. Pin the bird to the pink background piece. Use one-ply floss to blanketstitch around the bird. Embroider the wing using the chainstitch and the herringbone stitch. Blanketstitch the wing to the bird and embroider the bird's feathers. Use one-ply floss to chainstitch the looped and wavy vine around the bird and stitch the leaves.

Follow steps 3, 4, and 5 on page 59.

Owl Purse

Materials

* Wool felt: one 4½"x 10½" piece blue for purse, one 3" x 4" piece yellow for background, one 3" x 3" piece lavender for owl
* Five green 6mm glass beads
* Two small white buttons for eyes

DIRECTIONS

Follow Step 1 on page 59.

BLUEBIRD PURSE

Pin the owl to the yellow background piece. Use one-ply floss to blanket stitch around the owl outside edge. Embroider the owl, including the head, feathers, and claws, with chain stitch and fly stitch. Sew on the button eyes, and embroider the beak with satin stitch. Use one-ply floss to chain-stitch the looped and wavy vine around the owl. Sew on the beads.

Follow Steps 4 and 5 on page 59.

Oak Leaf Purse

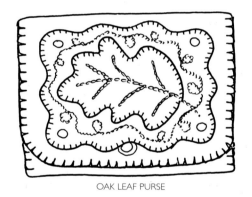
OAK LEAF PURSE

Materials

* Wool felt: one 4½" x 10½" piece lavender for purse, one 3" x 4" piece orange for background, one 3" x 3" piece light green for oak leaf
* 4 small, round nail heads

DIRECTIONS

Follow Step 1 on page 59.

Pin the oak leaf to the orange background piece. Use one-ply floss to blanketstitch around the leaf's outside edge. Chainstitch the stem and veins on the leaf. Use one-ply floss to chainstitch the looped and wavy vine around the leaf.

Follow Steps 3, 4, and 5 on page 59.

Butterfly Purse

BUTTERFLY PURSE

Materials

* Wool felt: one 4½" x 10½" piece orange for purse, one 3" x 4" piece blue for background, one 3" x 3" piece yellow for butterfly
* Beads: one 15mm tube, one 5mm round glass
* Six small, round nail heads

DIRECTIONS

Follow Step 1 on page 59.

Attach two nail heads to the butterfly's lower wing. Pin the butterfly to the blue background piece. Use one-ply floss to blanketstitch around the butterfly's outside edge. Embroider the wings with chain stitch, straight stitch, and French knots. Sew the tube bead and the round bead to the center of the butterfly to form the body. Use one-ply floss to chainstitch the looped and wavy vine around the butterfly.

Follow Steps 3, 4, and 5 on page 59.

Purse Patterns

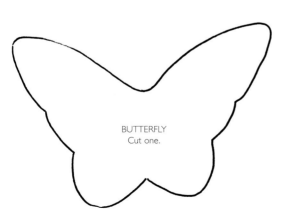

BUTTERFLY
Cut one.

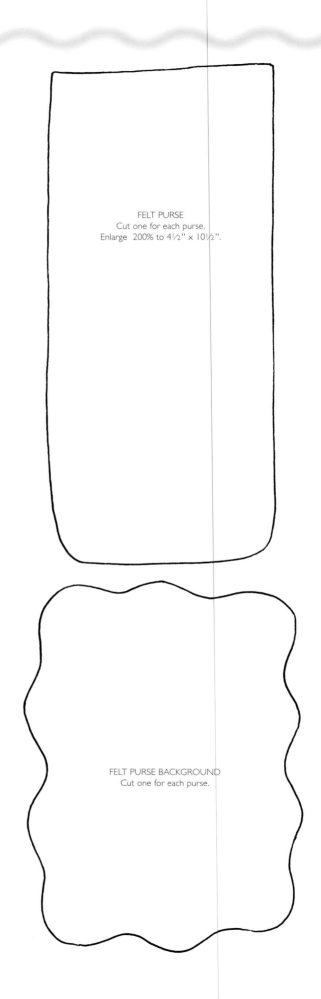

FELT PURSE
Cut one for each purse.
Enlarge 200% to 4½" x 10½".

FELT PURSE BACKGROUND
Cut one for each purse.

STRAW HAT
Cut one.

BLUE BIRD
Cut one.

BLUE BIRD WING
Cut one.

OAK LEAF
Cut one.

OWL
Cut one.

LAMB
Cut one.

LAMB'S EAR
Cut two.

CAT
Cut one.

MITTEN
Cut one.

Checkbook Holder and Cell Phone Cover

Elephant Checkbook Holder

Finished size: 3¼" × 6¼"

CHECKBOOK HOLDER AND CELL PHONE COVER,
Photo by Doug Mindell

To make the checkbook holder or the cell phone cover shown in the photograph, follow the basic directions, adjusting as necessary for shapes, materials, and stitches unique to each design. Any of the pin patterns on pages 56-57 can also be enlarged and used for appliqué designs. Refer to the photograph for colors, locations of items, and stitching ideas. Small beads can be substituted for nail heads. The most frequently used stitch is the blanket stitch, with French knots, chain stitch, and herringbone stitch adding colorful details. *Because the checkbook holder and cell phone cover have small parts, they are not intended for use by children under age 3.*

Materials

(Specific materials are listed for individual projects.)

* Wool felt
* Nail heads
* Size 3 perle cotton thread
* Embroidery floss
* Embroidery needle
* Needle-nosed pliers

Materials

* Wool felt: one 13" × 14" piece red for outside and inside panels, one 3" × 4½" piece gray for elephant body, one 1½" × 2" piece green for blanket, one ¾" × 6¾" piece blue and one ¾" × 6¾" piece green for side strips
* Nine small, round nail heads

1. Using patterns on page 66, cut out pieces from wool felt. Enlarge the pattern as necessary to fit your checkbook.
2. Blanketstitch the outside curve of the elephant's ear and then continue the stitches along the straight side, attaching the ear to the body. Attach a nail head for the elephant's eye. Decorate with straight stitches and blanketstitch the blanket onto the elephant's back. Stitch the elephant's mouth with straight stitches.

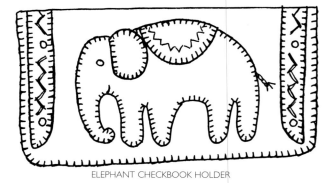

ELEPHANT CHECKBOOK HOLDER

3. Attach nail heads to the side strips by pushing the prongs through the felt and then with needle-nosed pliers bend the prongs on the underside. Use two-ply floss to embroider the zigzag design with herringbone stitches. Blanketstitch the side strips to the checkbook holder, 1/4'' in from the long cut edge.

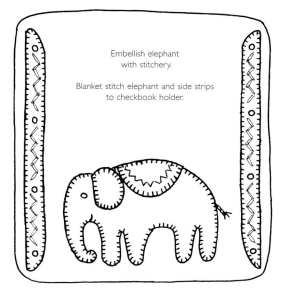

Embellish elephant with stitchery.

Blanket stitch elephant and side strips to checkbook holder.

4. Pin the elephant's body in place on the checkbook holder front, and with one-ply floss, blanketstitch around the outside edge of the body. Chainstitch a tail with two-ply floss, adding a few straight stitches that fan out at the end.

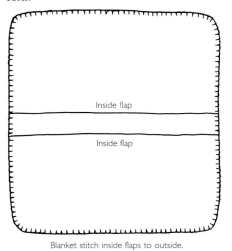

Inside flap

Inside flap

Blanket stitch inside flaps to outside.

5. Pin the two inside flaps to the holder wrong side. Use perle cotton to blanketstitch around the outside edge to join the inside panels to the outside panel.

Cell Phone Cover

Alter the basic pattern to custom fit any size cell phone. Measure the phone's middle and add 1'' sliding room. Divide that number in half and use it as the width measurement for the front and back cover pieces. To determine the cover length measurement, measure the phone length and add 1/2''. Mark the location of the antenna hole.

Antenna hole

OAK LEAF CELL PHONE COVER

Materials

* Wool felt: one 7'' x 9'' piece blue for front and back, one 3'' x 3'' piece green for leaf
* 3/4'' circle of hook-and-loop fastener
* Size 3 perle cotton thread
* Embroidery floss
* Embroidery needle
* Matching sewing thread

DIRECTIONS

Cut the pattern pieces from wool felt. Use two-ply floss to blanketstitch the leaf to the cell phone cover front. Use two-ply floss to chainstitch the stem and vein pattern onto the leaf and stitch a curly line around the leaf and along one curved outside flap. Sew the hook-and-loop circle to the wrong side of the back cover flap and at the top of the cover front. Use perle cotton to blanketstitch along the single layer top edge of the cover front and around the entire outside edge to attach the front and back covers. Stitch through both layers of felt on the pocket portion and through the single layer of the flap.

Checkbook Holder and Cell Phone Cover Patterns

Enlarge all patterns to fit your checkbook or cell phone.

OAK LEAF STITCHING PATTERN

ELEPHANT EAR
Cut one.

LEAF (CELL PHONE COVER)
Cut one.

ELEPHANT SADDLE
Cut one.

Antenna Hole

CELL PHONE COVER BACK
Cut one 3" × 8½" rectangle.
Round off all corners as shown.
Mark antenna hole.

CHECKBOOK HOLDER SIDE STRIP
Cut two.

CHECKBOOK HOLDER OUTSIDE
Cut one 6¼" × 6¾" rectangle,
Round off all corners as shown.

CELL PHONE COVER FRONT
Cut one 3" × 6" rectangle.
Round off two corners as shown.

CHECKBOOK HOLDER INSIDE FLAP
Cut two 2¾" × 6¼" rectangles.
Round off two corners as shown.

ELEPHANT
Cut one.

Balsam Pillows

With soft wool felt, comforting imagery, and soothing aromatic balsam fir, these pillows bring pleasure through many senses. You can cuddle and squeeze them up, and inhale their distinctive balsam fragrance. If you prefer, use wool fleece instead of balsam fir to stuff them; beads can be substituted for nail heads. Omit choking hazards like beads and jingle bells to adapt designs for use by young children. To make any of the pillows shown in the photograph, follow the specific directions for each version and refer to the photograph for colors, item locations, and stitching ideas.

DIRECTIONS

To attach nail heads, push the prongs through the felt and use needle-nosed pliers to bend them over on the underside.

BALSAM PILLOWS, photo by Doug Mindell

Reindeer Pillow

Materials

* Wool felt: one 7½'' x 7½'' piece red for back, one 6½'' x 6½'' piece green for front, one piece 4½'' x 4½'' red for reindeer
* Five star nail heads
* Four small jingle bells
* Eight glass heart beads for leaves
* Small, size 6/0 round bead for eye
* Nine metallic seed beads

* Solid and variegated Wildflowers® cotton thread
* Embroidery needle
* Needle-nosed pliers
* Balsam fir

REINDEER PILLOW

DIRECTIONS

1. Cut patterns from wool felt. Pin the reindeer piece in place on the green pillow front. Blanketstitch around the reindeer's outside edge. Chainstitch the curled antler design. Sew on the bead eye and decorate the reindeer's body with French knots, chainstitched squiggles, fly stitches, and seed beads. Attach the star nail heads. Chainstitch a curled vine beneath the reindeer and sew on bead leaves. Use chainstitch and straight stitches to make the fir branches.

2. Blanketstitch the edge of the scalloped pillow back. Pin the pillow front onto the pillow back and blanketstitch around three sides. Through the open side, fill the pocket with firmly packed balsam fir. Continue blanketstitching the remaining edge closed.

Heart Pillow
Materials

* Wool felt: one 6'' x 7'' piece pink for back, one 5½'' x 6½'' piece lavender for front, one 3½'' x 4'' piece fuchsia for middle heart, one 2½'' x 3'' piece orange for inside heart
* Red ribbon rosette
* 14 small, round, red nail heads
* Solid and variegated Wildflowers cotton thread
* Embroidery needle
* Needle-nosed pliers
* Balsam fir

HEART PILLOW

DIRECTIONS

1. Cut patterns from wool felt. Use the inner line as a guide to cut out the inside of the small orange heart. Pin or baste the small orange heart onto the fuchsia heart piece and blanketstitch around the outer and inner edges. Chainstitch a wavy line and spirals on the fuchsia heart. Sew a rosette to the center of the heart. Blanketstitch the layered heart to the lavender heart around the outside edge. Chainstitch a wavy red outline around the heart. Attach the nail heads.

2. Blanketstitch around the scalloped heart back. Pin the front heart to the back heart. Blanketstitch around the front heart, leaving a 2'' opening. Through the opening, fill the pillow with firmly packed balsam fir. Continue blanketstitching the opening closed.

Gingerbread Cookies Pillow
Materials

* Wool felt: two 9'' x 11'' pieces blue for front and back, one 4½'' x 7½'' piece red for border corners, one 4'' x 6'' piece green for top and bottom and side borders, one 4'' x 5'' piece green for holly leaves, one 2'' x 2½'' piece pink for mitten, one 2½'' x 2½'' piece yellow for star, one 2'' x 2'' piece red for heart, one 4½'' x 6½'' piece brown for gingerbread cookies
* Nail heads: 4 stars, 9 small red circles for holly berries, one large circle for star center, 35 small, round for border
* Twelve small, size 6/0 dark brown beads for gingerbread cookies
* Threads: metallic embroidery floss; size 3 Perle cotton
* Embroidery needle
* Needle-nosed pliers

GINGERBREAD COOKIE PILLOW

DIRECTIONS

1. Cut two 8½'' x 10½'' pieces of blue wool felt for the pillow front and back and round off the corners as shown. Cut patterns from felt. Chainstitch the squiggly outline onto the gingerbread cookies. Sew on the bead eyes and buttons. Decorate the mitten, heart, star, and holly leaves with herringbone, chain, fly, blanket, and straight stitch embroidery. Pin the felt pieces in place on the front pillow piece. Blanket stitch around the outside edges of all pieces. Chainstitch the curled lines onto the pillow. Attach the nail heads.

2. Use perle cotton to blanketstitch the scalloped edges of the pillow border pieces. Pin or baste the border sections in place under the pillow front. Use perle cotton to blanketstitch around the outer front edge, attaching the border sections to the pillow front. Pin or baste the pillow back in place. Use perle cotton to blanketstitch around the outer edge of the back, leaving a 4'' opening. Stuff with firmly packed balsam fir and blanketstitch to close.

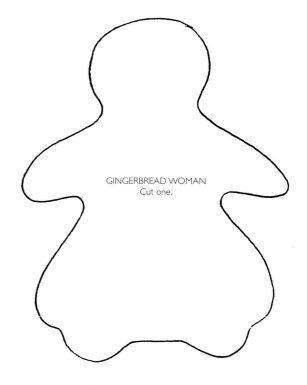

GINGERBREAD WOMAN
Cut one.

Balsam Pillow Patterns

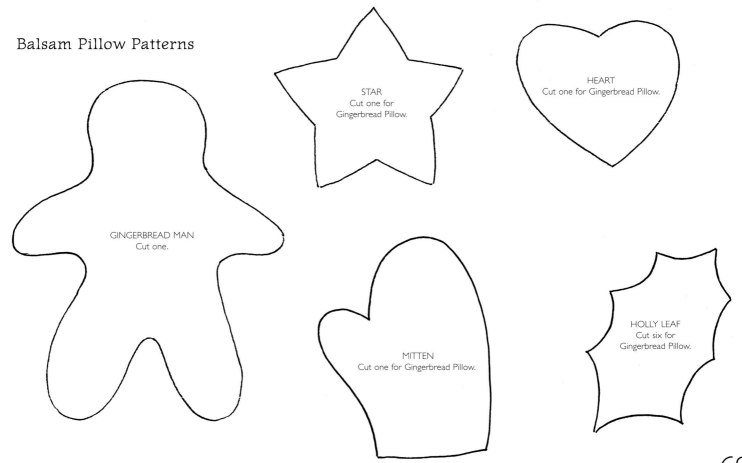

GINGERBREAD MAN
Cut one.

STAR
Cut one for
Gingerbread Pillow.

HEART
Cut one for Gingerbread Pillow.

MITTEN
Cut one for Gingerbread Pillow.

HOLLY LEAF
Cut six for
Gingerbread Pillow.

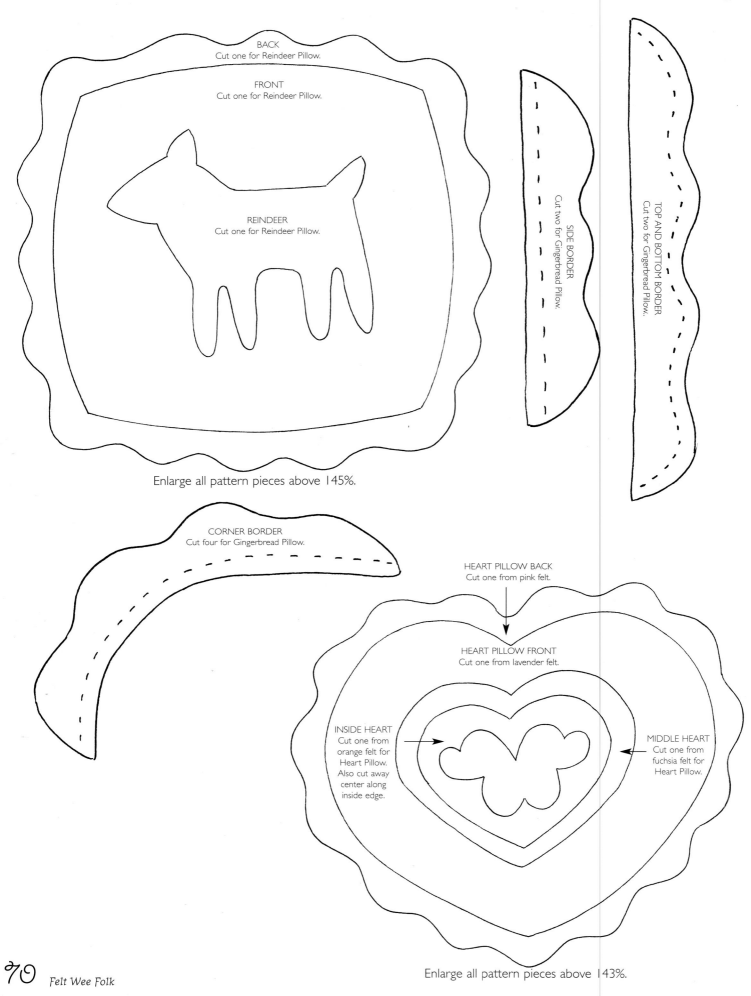

BACK
Cut one for Reindeer Pillow.

FRONT
Cut one for Reindeer Pillow.

REINDEER
Cut one for Reindeer Pillow.

SIDE BORDER
Cut two for Gingerbread Pillow.

TOP AND BOTTOM BORDER
Cut two for Gingerbread Pillow.

Enlarge all pattern pieces above 145%.

CORNER BORDER
Cut four for Gingerbread Pillow.

HEART PILLOW BACK
Cut one from pink felt.

HEART PILLOW FRONT
Cut one from lavender felt.

INSIDE HEART
Cut one from orange felt for Heart Pillow. Also cut away center along inside edge.

MIDDLE HEART
Cut one from fuchsia felt for Heart Pillow.

Enlarge all pattern pieces above 143%.

Fabric Relief Projects

These two projects feature appliquéd wool felt back-grounds that create permanent settings for the attached Wee Folk. The finished felt panels may be mounted on fabric and framed. Other embellishments enhance the scene, including glass leaves, flower and seed beads, and embroidered details complete the picture. There is much opportunity to experiment with different embroidery stitches and use a variety of colored threads.

Plant-dyed wool felt is used in the featured examples. The threads are DMC embroidery floss and silk, cotton and silk/wool threads from the Caron Collection.

PUPPY PLAY, photo by Doug Mindell

Puppy Play

Finished size: 9" × 12"

Materials

* 8" × 11" piece navy blue wool felt for the background
* 2" × 7" piece light green wool felt for the garden panel
* 3" × 7" piece medium green wool felt for the grassy hill
* 7" × 7" piece light blue wool felt for the sky and boy's shirt
* 8" × 10" piece orange wool felt for the house and borders
* 2½" × 3" piece brown wool felt for the tree
* ¼" × 4½" strip yellow wool felt for the roof of the house
* 3" × 3" piece lavender wool felt for house windows and girl's shirt
* 1¼" × 2" piece mustard wool felt for girl's skirt
* 2" × 3" piece tan wool felt for dog and boy's pants
* 1" × 1½" piece medium blue wool felt for house door
* 4½" small size rickrack for house
* Three 25mm plastic grape leaf beads
* Three 12mm glass green flower beads
* Eight 9mm glass heart leaf beads
* Six small 6/0 glass blue beads
* Two yellow/gold glass flower beads
* Eight 8mm glass oval leaf beads
* Nine 13mm × 9mm glass leaf beads for tree
* Ten yellow seed beads for bushes
* Metallic seed bead for doorknob
* ¼" bead for chimney
* Two 12mm unvarnished wooden beads
* Two acorn caps to fit the beads
* Small wad wool fleece for hair
* Small wad wool fleece for dog stuffing
* Three 12"-long, 3mm diameter chenille stems
* Embroidery floss
* Embroidery needle
* Cotton, silk, or wool/silk thread
* Variegated colored thread

DIRECTIONS

Refer to the photograph for color selection, placement of felt pieces, and location of beads, embroidery stitches, and figures.

Patterns

Round the upper corners and use the dashed line on the bottom border pattern as a guide to cut three waves at the lower edge of the 8" × 11" navy blue background piece. Use the patterns on pages 73–75 to cut out the sky, grassy hill, garden panel, house, roof, tree, windows, door, and scalloped border pieces from appropriate wool felt colors.

House Blanketstitch the door and windows to the house front. Chainstitch the door and window windowpanes and the plants under the windows. Sew yellow seed beads to plant stems. Create texture on the upper portion of the house with several lines of blanketstitches. Sew rickrack to the house roof peak, turning under the raw ends. Blanketstitch the sides and lower edge of the house. Use small blanketstitches to edge the roof. Sew the roof to the top of the house. Add bead for doorknob.

PUPPY PLAY
Sky, Grassy Hill, House, Tree Embellishment

GARDEN PANEL EMBELLISHMENT

Grassy Hill/Sky Position the grassy hill and sky pieces together and pin or baste in place. Blanket-stitch along the top edge of the grassy hill piece, attaching it to the sky piece. Blanketstitch the lower section of the hill and the sides and top of the sky.

Tree Position and sew the tree to the sky/grassy hill piece, using small blanket stitches around the outer edges of the trunk and branches. Sew leaf beads to the tree branches. Sew the house to the sky/grassy hill piece. Sew on bead chimney.

Decorate the grassy hill and sky with chain-stitch swirls. Use single daisy stitches to create blades of grass in the leafy design around the grassy hill swirls and on the sky piece close to the top of the grassy hill.

Garden Panel Finish the outside edge of the garden panel piece with small blanket stitches. Use chain stitches to embroider curlicues and swirls. Sew on flower and leaf beads. Embroider daisy stitches around the bead flowers.

Background and Scalloped Border Blanket-stitch the outer edges of the wool felt background and the outer edges of the scalloped border pieces. Sew the border pieces in place under the background.

Position the sky/grassy hill and garden panel pieces on the background and pin or baste in place. Sew the sections to the background around the out-side edges. Blend the stitches with previously blanket-stitched edges. Outline the appliquéd panels with wavy, curled chain-stitched lines. Make flowers with beads, daisy-stitched petals and chain-stitched stems. Add chain-stitched vines and squiggles to the lower portion and sew on leaf beads.

Boy, Girl, and Dog Cut out doll clothes and dog patterns from wool felt. Make a boy and girl by following directions on page 27 for the 2½'' doll. The dog is made by wrapping a 3mm chenille stem with six strands of embroidery floss to create an armature with four legs and a tail. After wrapping the legs and tail, knot the thread end and trim. Bend the stem ends inward to conform to the dog's shape.

Begin joining the dog front and back together by blanketstitching around the head and back. Insert the armature into the dog's body, leaving the wrapped legs and tail sticking out. Stuff the head and body with a small amount of fleece and finish stitching. Sew on the dog's ear and embroider an eye, nose, mouth, and collar. Attach the boy, girl, and dog to the background, securing their legs and bodies in place with a few stitches.

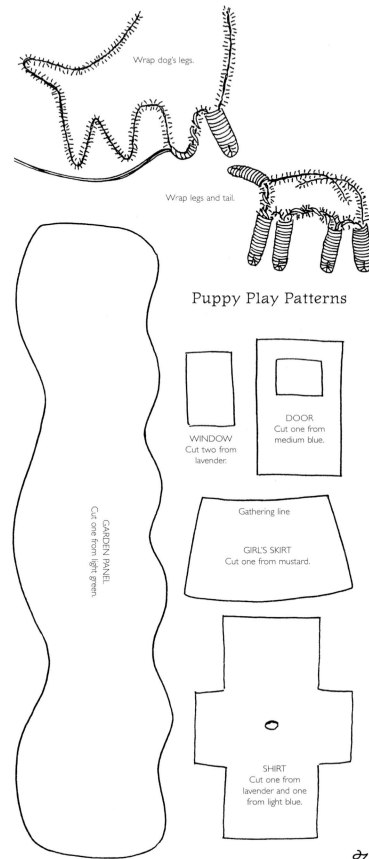

Wrap dog's legs.

Wrap legs and tail.

Puppy Play Patterns

WINDOW
Cut two from lavender.

DOOR
Cut one from medium blue.

Gathering line

GIRL'S SKIRT
Cut one from mustard.

GARDEN PANEL
Cut one from light green.

SHIRT
Cut one from lavender and one from light blue.

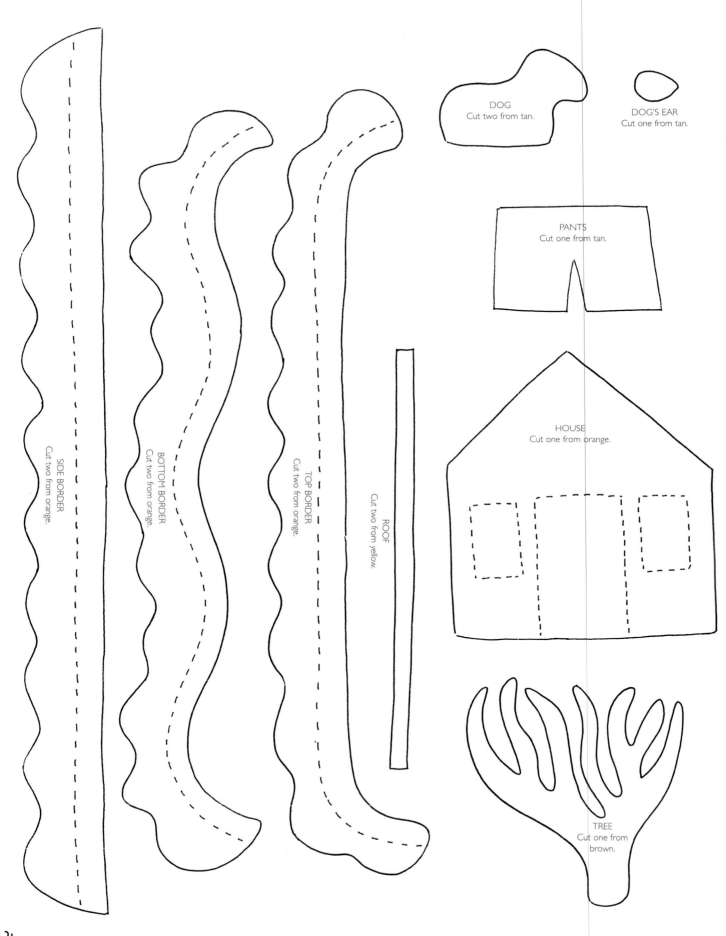

DOG
Cut two from tan.

DOG'S EAR
Cut one from tan.

PANTS
Cut one from tan.

HOUSE
Cut one from orange.

SIDE BORDER
Cut two from orange.

BOTTOM BORDER
Cut two from orange.

TOP BORDER
Cut two from orange.

ROOF
Cut two from yellow.

TREE
Cut one from brown.

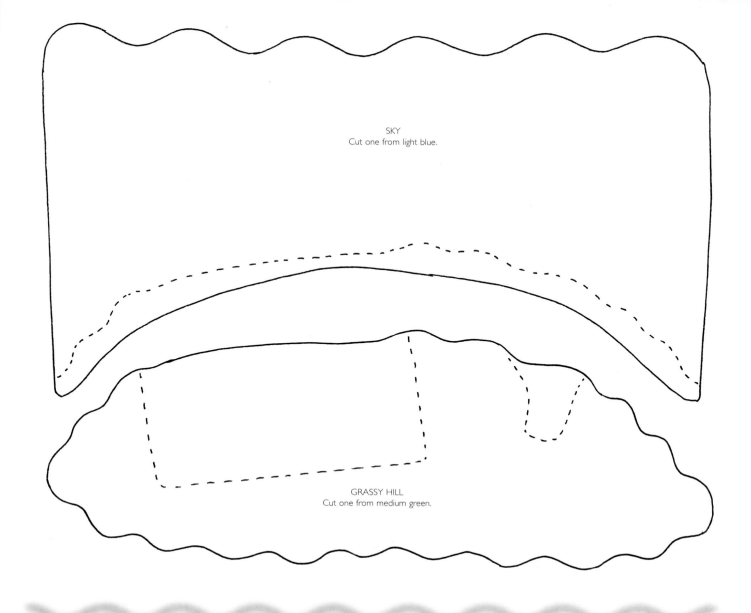

SKY
Cut one from light blue.

GRASSY HILL
Cut one from medium green.

Fall Fairy

Finished Size: 8'' x 8''

Materials

* 7'' x 7'' piece medium green wool felt for the background
* 5'' x 7½'' piece medium blue wool felt for borders
* 2'' x 3''piece light green wool felt for Leaf 3
* 2'' x 2'' piece olive green wool felt for Leaf 1
* 1½'' x 2½'' piece pastel green wool felt for fairy tunic
* 4'' x 4'' piece orange wool felt for Leaves 2, 4, 5, 6, and 7
* Six size 6/0 aqua glass beads
* Six size 6/0 wine glass beads

* 32-gauge cloth-covered spool wire (approx. 70'')
* 2½'' doll armature (page 27)
* 12mm unvarnished wooden bead for head
* Acorn cap to fit the bead
* Wad of wool fleece for hair
* Artificial freesia flower for wings
* Artificial flower petals for fairy skirt
* Embroidery floss
* Embroidery needle
* Variegated silk thread
* Cotton thread

Refer to the illustrations for making the leaves. Refer to the photograph for color selection, placement of felt pieces, and location of beads, embroidery stitches, and the fairy.

Background Round off the corners of the 7'' x 7'' green felt background piece and blanketstitch the outside edges. Cut out border pieces from medium blue felt and blanketstitch along the scalloped edges. Sew the border pieces in place under all four sides of the background piece.

Chainstitch a continuous, squiggly vine around the outer edge of the green background. Use variegated thread to make tiny leaves along the vine with single daisy stitches. Chainstitch berry branches and sew on glass beads.

Leaves Cut leaf patterns out of felt. Attach cloth-covered wire to the outside edge of the large orange oak leaf by sewing a compact satin stitch around both the wire and felt. Completely cover both to make a smooth, finished leaf edge. Hide the wire ends by bending them under the leaf. To make the leaf stem, bend an 8''-section of cloth-covered wire in half. Use three-ply floss to wrap the bent end, covering the wire. Squeeze the wire ends together and wrap embroidery floss around 2'' of the double wire. Cover the thread ends as you wind the thread. Use the same floss to join the stem to the leaf along the center. Wind the thread around the wire as you attach it to the felt leaf, covering the wire completely and making a neat, smooth stem line.

The smaller leaves are not edged with wire but do have wire stems. Finish the outside edges of the leaves with a compact satin stitch. Wrap the wire stems the same way as for the large leaf and adjust the wire length to fit the smaller leaves. Attach the stems and finish the leaves with detailed embroidery.

Fairy Make the fairy by following the directions for a 2½'' fairy on page 27. Bend the wire edges of the large oak leaf to form an inviting place to snooze. Sew the fairy in place. Attach all of the leaves to the background with a few stitches along the center stems.

NOTE: When painting the doll's face, make eyes closed, as if sleeping.

FALL FAIRY, photo by Doug Mindell

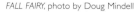

Fall Fairy Patterns

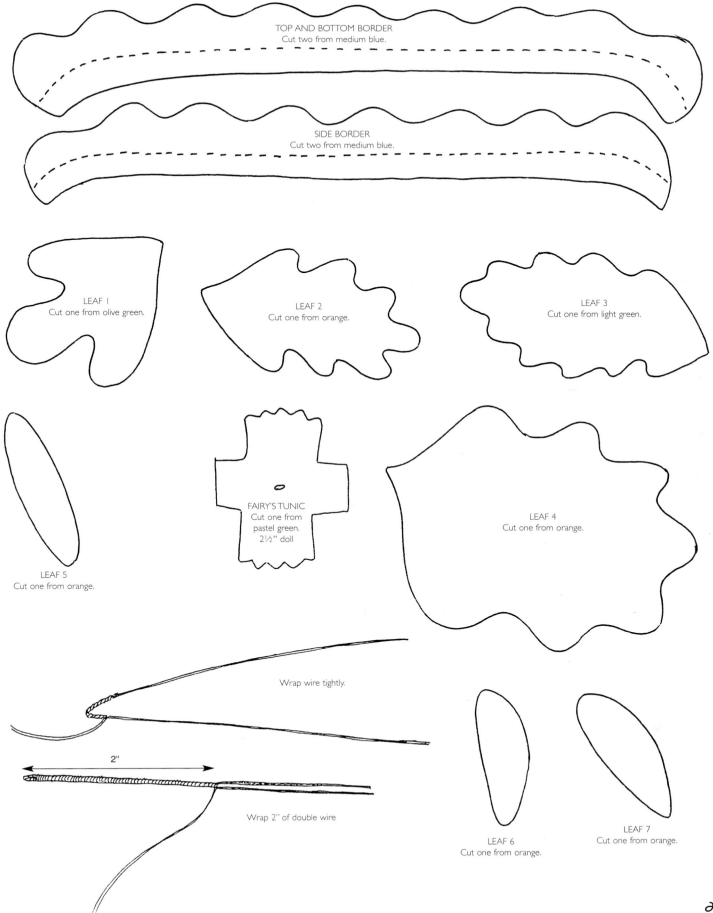

TOP AND BOTTOM BORDER
Cut two from medium blue.

SIDE BORDER
Cut two from medium blue.

LEAF 1
Cut one from olive green.

LEAF 2
Cut one from orange.

LEAF 3
Cut one from light green.

LEAF 5
Cut one from orange.

FAIRY'S TUNIC
Cut one from pastel green.
2½" doll

LEAF 4
Cut one from orange.

Wrap wire tightly.

2"

Wrap 2" of double wire

LEAF 6
Cut one from orange.

LEAF 7
Cut one from orange.

Glossary of Stitches

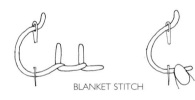

BLANKET STITCH

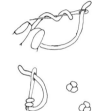

CHAIN STITCH

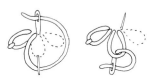

DAISY STITCH

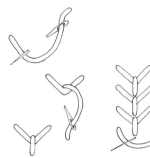

FLY STITCH

FRENCH KNOT

HERRINGBONE STITCH

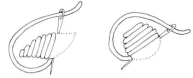

SATIN STITCH

STRAIGHT STITCH

Sources

THREADS
The Caron Collection, (203) 381-9999, Website www.caron-net.com

Perle cotton and embroidery floss, DMC Corp., South Hackensack Ave., Port Kearny Bldg. 10A, South Kearny, NJ 07032. To order DMC products by mail, contact Herrschners (800) 441-0838, Website www.herrschners.com

BUTTONS
Bird and other novelty buttons, JHB International, (303) 751-8100, Website www.buttons.com

CRAFT SUPPLIES
Chenille stems and nail heads, Westrim Crafts, 9667 Canoga Ave., Chatsworth, CA 91311, Tel. (818) 998-8550, Website www.westrimcrafts.com

FAUX FLOWERS
Jo Ann Fabrics and Crafts, (888) 739-4120, Website www.joann.com

BEADS, SNAPS, NAIL HEADS
Glass and clear plastic beads: The Bead Tree, P.O. Box 682, West Falmouth, MA 02574, (508) 548-4665, Website www.thebeadtree.com

Unvarnished wooden beads: Woodworks, P.O. Box 161129, Fort Worth, TX 76161, (800)722-0311

Glass beads: Beads by Mail, P.O. Box 227, Pembroke, MA 02359, (800) 572-7920, Website www.beadsbymail.com

East of Oz, P.O. Box 665, Bronx, NY 10469, (718) 798-7961, Website www.eastofoz.com

Snap fasteners and nail heads: The Bee Lee Company, P.O. Box 36108, Dallas, TX 75235, (800)527-5271

Nail Heads: Eisen/EMCO, Inc., 462 Barell Ave., Carlstadt, NJ 07072, (201) 939-1870, Website www.nailheads.com

WOOL FELT AND FLEECE
Plant-dyed wool felt and fleece: Creative Hands, P.O. Box 2217, Eugene, OR 97402, (541) 343-1562

Wool felt and fleece: Magic Cabin Dolls, (888) 623-6557, Website www.magiccabin.com

Plant-dyed wool felt and fleece: A Child's Dream Come True, P.O. Box 163, Sandpoint, ID 83864, (800) 359-2906, Website www.achildsdream.com

Plant-dyed wool felt: Earthsong Fibers, 5115 Excelsior Blvd. #428, Minneapolis, MN 55416, (800) 473-5350, Website www.earthsongfibers.com

Wool felt: Nova Natural, 817 Chestnut Ridge Rd., Chestnut Ridge, NY 10977, (877) 668-2111 Website www.novanatural.com

Wool felts, National Nonwovens, P.O. Box 150, Easthampton, MA 01027, (800) 333-3469, Website www.woolfelt.com

BALSAM
Maine Balsam Fir, P.O. Box 9, 16 Morse Hill Rd., West Paris, ME 04289, (800) 522-5726, Website www.mainebalsam.com

About the Author

Photo by Rob Goldsborough

Salley Mavor grew up in the seaside village of Woods Hole, Massachusetts in a household full of treasures and creative ideas. She learned to sew as a child and has been playing with a needle and thread ever since. At home, there were always art supplies close at hand and a sense that time was available for creative pursuit. Drawing with crayons was never enough for Salley. She remembers feeling that her work was not finished until something real was glued, stapled or sewn to it.

A graduate of the Rhode Island School of Design, Ms. Mavor has illustrated six children's books using her unique blend of materials and techniques, including *In the Heart*, written by Ann Turner and the classic *Mary Had a Little Lamb*. She now designs sewing kits and note cards for her business, Wee Folk Studio, and lives with her husband, Rob Goldsborough and their sons, Peter and Ian, in Falmouth, Massachusetts.

Salley Mavor's kits and note cards are available from:

Wee Folk Studio
P.O. Box 152
Woods Hole, MA 02543
www.weefolkstudio.com

Index

OTHER FINE BOOKS FROM C&T PUBLISHING

For more information write for a free catalog:
C&T Publishing, Inc.
P.O. Box 1456
Lafayette, CA 94549
(800) 284-1114
E-mail: ctinfo@ctpub.com
Website: www.ctpub.com

For supplies:
Cotton Patch Mail Order
3405 Hall Lane, Dept. CTB
Lafayette, CA 94549
(800) 835-4418
(925) 283-7883
E-mail: quiltusa@yahoo.com
Website: www.quiltusa.com